◎本书获得湖南第一师范学院外国语学院英语与翻译省级一流

◎本书为湖南省哲学社会科学基金项目"基于混合方法的小学
究"（18YBA098）的结题成果之一。

U0687171

中小学英语教师
语言评价素养研究

贺满足 / 著

N

P

R

Q

S

湖南师范大学出版社

·长沙·

图书在版编目(CIP)数据

中小学英语教师语言评价素养研究 / 贺满足著. —长沙:湖南师范大学出版社,2023.1

ISBN 978-7-5648-4757-9

Ⅰ.①中… Ⅱ.①贺… Ⅲ.①中小学—英语—教师评价—研究 Ⅳ.①G633.412

中国版本图书馆 CIP 数据核字(2022)第 212702 号

中小学英语教师语言评价素养研究
Study of Primary and Middle School EFL Teachers' Language Assessment Literacy

贺满足 著

◇出 版 人:吴真文
◇策划组稿:李 阳
◇责任编辑:李永芳 李 阳
◇责任校对:李 航
◇出版发行:湖南师范大学出版社
　　　　　地址/长沙市岳麓区 邮编/410081
　　　　　电话/0731-88872256 0731-88873070
　　　　　网址/https://press.hunnu.edu.cn
◇经销:新华书店
◇印刷:长沙市宏发印刷有限公司
◇开本:710 mm×1000 mm 1/16
◇印张:14.75
◇字数:300 千字
◇版次:2023 年 1 月第 1 版
◇印次:2023 年 1 月第 1 次印刷
◇书号:ISBN 978-7-5648-4757-9
◇定价:69.00 元

凡购本书,如有缺页、倒页、脱页,由本社发行部调换。

投稿热线:0731-88872256 微信:ly13975805626 QQ:1349748847

Abstract

The study reported in this book investigated language assessment literacy (LAL) in the Chinese educational context. It aims to: (1) conceptualize a body of assessment knowledge and skills prerequisite for Chinese primary and middle school English as a foreign language (EFL) teachers; (2) construct a reliable and valid instrument to measure EFL teachers' LAL; and (3) examine these teachers' current LAL levels. A mixed-methods approach was employed to collect data. Qualitative data sources included professional standards for teachers, prominent assessment standards, self-structured interviews, and open-ended questionnaire surveys. Quantitative data included those collected from questionnaire surveys in the piloting, formal and follow-up studies.

The construct of LAL for Chinese primary and middle school EFL teachers was defined in a comprehensive way based on literature review, analysis of standards documents, and feedback from experienced EFL teachers and domain experts. Built upon this definition, an LAL model was developed and its validity was established through several stages of expert judgement. This model, framed within a "skills+knowledge+principles" approach, included five components, i. e. knowledge of assessment in language pedagogy, knowledge of linguistics and applied linguistics, awareness of students' cognitive and affective characteristics, technical skills in assessment, and assessment principles & ethic considerations. Built on the LAL model, a measuring instrument was constructed to assess Chinese EFL teachers' LAL levels. The development of the instrument underwent several stages, including a thorough review of existent studies, creating an item pool, seeking experts' feedback, and piloting. Analysis of the data from the second piloting showed the instrument had desirable psychometric properties and a factor structure commensurate with the component structure of the LAL model.

The final form of the questionnaire consisted of 62 items and was administered online to EFL teachers. A total of 835 primary and middle school EFL teachers (mostly from Hunan and Guangdong provinces) completed the survey, and 439 participants' responses were retained for statistical analysis. Exploratory factor analysis of the data showed that the items in the instrument had a factor structure quite similar to that identified in the second piloting, lending further support to the construct validity of the LAL measuring instrument. This questionnaire could thus serve as a valid and reliable instrument to assess Chinese EFL teachers' LAL.

Descriptive statistics showed that EFL teachers had a basic LAL level. Yet, they had varied competence in different LAL areas. Specifically, they reported adequate literacy in awareness of students' cognitive and affective characteristics and assessment principles & ethic considerations, basic levels in assessment in language pedagogy and technical skills in assessment, but rather inadequate competence in knowledge of linguistics and applied linguistics.

Demographic factors were found to be related to LAL levels in different ways. ANOVA test showed grade levels of teaching had no significant effect on EFL teachers' overall LAL and competence in LAL areas at the .05 level, except for the dimension of knowledge of linguistics and applied linguistics. Specifically, senior middle school EFL teachers reported significantly higher levels of knowledge of linguistics and applied linguistics than EFL teachers from primary and junior middle schools, and junior middle school EFL teachers also reported significantly better knowledge than primary EFL teachers. The institutional context was also found to be related to EFL teachers' knowledge of linguistics and applied linguistics. EFL teachers in urban and county town schools had significantly better knowledge than teachers in rural areas, but there was no significant difference between teachers from these two institutional contexts. Assessment training, however, was a significant factor that affected EFL teachers' overall LAL and their competence in LAL areas except for awareness of students' cognitive and affective characteristics.

The research findings have implications for theory, policy, and practice. An LAL construct needs to underscore situation-specific principles, values, and particularly the traditions in a specific culture. The reported basic levels of literacy warrant the need to improve the LAL of EFL teachers. The successful improvement of EFL teachers' LAL is contingent on a multitude of factors. At the macro level, policymakers need to stipulate supportive assessment policies, educational assessment standards, guidelines, and codes of ethics to guide sound assessment practices. At the meso level, initial teacher education programs need to give curricular prominence to AL/LAL via discrete (language) assessment courses. For assessment training to be effective, the training programs need to plan the topics and training methods based on in-service EFL teachers' practical needs. At the micro level, EFL teachers' attitudes toward and beliefs about assessment are vital in promoting competence in assessment. They need to realize the pedagogical power of assessment in facilitating student learning.

The current research makes several contributions to the existent literature. First, it addresses a research gap by conceptualizing LAL in the Chinese educational context and developing a model of LAL appropriate for primary and middle school EFL teachers. Teacher education programs could utilize this model as a reference to offer courses to prepare pre-service teachers for effective assessment practices. Second, a reliable and valid LAL measuring instrument was constructed. This instrument might be used to identify the needs of in-service EFL teachers and to develop appropriate training programs. Third, statistical analyses were conducted to investigate whether differences existed in LAL levels among EFL teachers working at different levels of instruction.

Admittedly, there are some inadequacies in the LAL conceptualization and the measuring instrument. Another limitation lies in the generalizability of the research findings by the use of a non-random sampling technique in the formal questionnaire survey with respondents generally from two provinces. A further limitation is investigating EFL teachers' LAL in isolation from their conceptions of assessment.

Recommendations for further studies include cooperating with representatives of other disciplines in establishing an LAL model and more empirical research for construct validation of the instrument with the use of more robust statistical analysis. In the meantime, there remains a need to investigate the appropriateness of the instrument for measuring pre-service EFL teachers' LAL levels.

Keywords: language assessment literacy, primary and middle school EFL teachers, conceptualization, LAL model, measuring instrument

Acknowledgements

My sincere gratitude and great appreciation are first expressed to my doctoral supervisor Prof. Liu Jianda for his ongoing constructive feedback. I have gained enormously from his knowledge, skills, and encouragement. If it had not been for his constant guidance and support, this book would not have been brought to its present form.

I owe special thanks to Prof. Cai Hongwen, who impresses me a lot with his profound knowledge and rigorous scholarship. He has been supportive of my study and provided me with much constructive feedback. I need to express my gratitude to the experts (e. g. Prof. Xu Yueting, Prof. Lin Dunlai, Prof. G. T. L. Brown, Dr. Harding), especially Prof. Yu Shengming, for their valuable feedback on the LAL conceptualization, theoretical model, and the measuring instrument.

I'd like to extend my sincere thanks to all those teachers, colleagues, former classmates, former and present students, friends, and others who provided me with great help in the collection and analysis of qualitative and quantitative data. The list is long, and here are only a few names: Prof. Yang Manzhen, Prof. Xiao Yunnan, Prof. Xiao Wei, associate Prof. Ouyang Lingli, Yang Huzhi, Dr. Zou Run, Guo Yingping, Liu Ping, Lv Lingyun, Wang Fang, Jiang Yancheng, Zheng Hui, Chang Wei, and She Zhenzhen.

My thanks also go to the leaders and colleagues in the Foreign Language Faculty of Hunan First Normal University for their support of the publication of this book. Special thanks go to Prof. Kang Xiangying, Prof.

Dai Shuijiao, and Dr. Wang Jiadi. Prof. Kang offered me great help in the selection of an appropriate publishing house, and Dr. Wang gave me valuable suggestions for revision before the book was finalized.

Sincere thanks also go to the editors in Hunan Normal University Press for their support in the whole revision process. I am grateful to Dr. Li Yang, the director of the editorial department, for his thoughtfulness, patience, and kindness.

At last, I would like to express my special thanks to my family. I am indebted to my parents-in-law, who would never hesitate to give me a hand when I am in need of help. I owe gratitude to my husband for his understanding, love, and unconditional support. I also need to express my thanks to my children, especially my daughter, whose sweet smiles are a cure for my anxiety in the course of writing this book.

He Manzu

February, 2023

Changsha, Hunan, China

List of Abbreviations

ACAI—Approaches to Classroom Assessment Instrument

AERA—American Educational Research Association

AfL—assessment for learning

AFT—American Federation of Teachers

AL/LAL—assessment literacy, language assessment literacy

ALI—Assessment Literacy Inventory

ALP—advanced language proficiency

ANOVA—analysis of variances

APA—American Psychological Association

ARG—assessment reform group

CAEP—Council for the Accreditation of Educator Preparation

CAL—classroom assessment literacy

CBSA—classroom-based summative assessment

CCSSO—Council of Chief State School Officers

CoA—conceptions of assessment

CSE—China's Standards of English Language Ability

CSNTP—Curriculum Standards for National Training Program

DoE—Department of Education

EFA—exploratory factor analysis

EFL—English as a foreign language

ESA—external summative assessment

FA—formative assessment/factor analysis

GTC—General Teaching Council

InTASC—Interstate Teacher Assessment and Support Consortium

JAC—Joint Advisory Committee

JCSEE—Joint Committee for Standards on Educational Evaluation

LSD—least squared difference

MoE—Ministry of Education

MoF—Ministry of Finance

NBPTS—National Board for Professional Teaching Standards

NCME—National Council on Measurement in Education

NCS—New Curriculum Standards

NEA—National Education Association

NMET—National Matriculation English Test

PCK—pedagogical content knowledge

PRC—People's Republic of China

RQ—research question

TALiP—teacher assessment literacy in practice

TCAQ—Teacher Competencies Assessment Questionnaire

TRA—Teaching Regulation Agency

Contents

CHAPTER ONE
INTRODUCTION TO THIS STUDY

1.1   Research Background

Due to the accountability and standards-based education reform, teachers are accountable to the public to provide evidence-based rationale for instructional and assessment decisions. Assessment of student learning has been recognized as an essential competency for teachers working within the current accountability educational context (Brookhart, 2001). Assessment practices rely on a core set of skills and specialized knowledge which, when applied, are a significant component of teacher effectiveness. Hence, teachers are expected to demonstrate knowledge of assessment purposes, learning objectives, and students' proficiency levels, and to use assessment data to differentiate instructions to move students forward toward their learning targets so that they can maximize the learning potential of assessment and monitor student progress in the meantime.

The discussion regarding teachers' competence in assessment has led to the emergence of the term "assessment literacy" (AL). Stiggins (1991) coined this term to refer to teachers' basic understanding of educational assessment and their ability to apply that knowledge in the assessment of student learning. Falsgraf (2006) interpreted AL as "... the ability to understand, analyze, and apply information on student performance to improve instruction" (p. 6). Volante and Fazio (2007) maintained that AL ought to be viewed as an integral part of teaching and learning, with teachers being accountable for students' learning outcomes. Shepard *et al.* (2005) articulated that:

> ... to be effective, teachers must be skillful in using various assessment strategies and tools and they have to have a deep understanding of the formative assessment process and understand its close relationship with instructional scaffolding. They have to be able to use insights from assessment to plan and revise instruction and to provide feedback that explicitly helps students see how to improve. (p. 1275)

Teachers' AL has become a topic of major concern for educators (Popham, 2004, 2011a). It is deemed as an important part of teacher professionalism (Abell & Siegel, 2011; Brookhart, 2011; Schafer, 1993) and has become a requirement for teachers' accreditation in some educational programs in the United States. The term AL also extends to the language testing and assessment community, with more and more research into the language assessment literacy (LAL) of language teachers. The growing interest in AL/LAL is due in large part to a recognition of the critical role that assessment plays in improving student learning (Black & Wiliam, 1998) and to the realization that teachers are key assessors in educational assessment (Leung, 2004). As a subordinate to AL, LAL is a relatively new inventory in the testing and assessment community, and its development is still in its infancy (Fulcher, 2012). Nevertheless, the past decade has witnessed a growing body of research in this new area, and studies have centered on the more planned and formal assessments at the secondary and tertiary education levels. Researchers have proposed different profiles or frameworks of LAL for EFL teachers, some of which are generic (e. g. Kremmel & Harding, 2020; Taylor, 2013; Xu & G. T.

L. Brown, 2016) and applicable to all EFL teachers with no account of the unique characteristics of students and assessment settings. Still, some other frameworks target a specific EFL teacher cohort, such as primary and middle school EFL teachers (e. g. Lan & Fan, 2019; D. L. Lin, 2019; Yan *et al.*, 2018), and college EFL teachers (e. g. Tao, 2014). Overall, these LAL frameworks are adaptations of existent models.

Regrettably, few studies have addressed specifically the LAL of EFL teachers in Chinese primary and middle schools (these teachers were referred to as EFL teachers collectively in this book for the sake of convenience). What assessment knowledge and skills does this particular population of EFL teachers need to possess to implement assessments in a competent and professional manner? What instrument can we use to assess the LAL of these teachers in a reliable and valid way? And what are the EFL teachers' current levels of literacy in language assessment? More research is needed in these areas. This study aims to add to the current literature by addressing these areas of concern.

1.2   Research Context

The Ministry of Education (MoE) of the People's Republic of China (PRC) has launched many policy initiatives to reform the country's education system. In 2001, the MoE initiated a new round of curriculum reform nationwide in response to national policies on educational reform to address the needs of economic and technological development and to solve problems in English education at different levels. In terms of basic education, the MoE (2001) promulgated *The Outline for Reforming Basic Education Curriculum* (*The Outline*, for short) to guide primary and middle school curriculum reform. ① Reforming testing and assessment

---

① Notice of MoE's Issuing of *The Outline for Reforming Basic Education Curriculum* (*Trial*) (Basic Education Document No. 17 [2001]).

methods was identified as one of the six goals of curriculum reform. *The Outline stressed the necessity of changes in teachers' assessment practices to promote students' mastery of various competencies.* Primary and middle school teachers need to move toward more social-constructive teaching approaches and adopt alternative forms of assessment to enhance students' higher-order thinking skills, real-world problem-solving skills, positive habits of mind, and communication skills. Additionally, teachers need to place more emphasis on the learning process rather than the learning outcome to help cultivate and inspire students' learning enthusiasm and confidence.

　　This round of curriculum reform advocates the establishment of a system of "assessment for development", which aims at students' all-round development consistent with the concept of formative assessment and assessment for learning. To facilitate effective implementation of the new assessment policy, the MoE promulgated *The Notice on Actively Promoting Assessment and Testing System Reform for Primary and Middle Schools* (*The Notice* for short) in December 2002,[①] which specified the purpose, content, and methods of testing and assessment practices. The core contents of *The Notice* were the specifications that primary and middle schools should put the assessment for learning reform at the heart of school education planning due to its proven benefits of facilitating student learning. Teachers were expected to obtain useful information about student learning to inform instructional planning and students could promote their learning with teachers' feedback.

　　In 2011, the MoE released a revised version of *The Outline*, i. e. *The New Curriculum Standards* (the NCS). A significant change in the revised version is related to the assessment component, with the focus shifting from

---

①　The Notice on Actively Promoting Assessment and Testing system Reform for Primary and Middle Schools (National Development Document No. 26[2002]).

building a system of formative assessment to optimizing assessment methods with a special emphasis on assessing students' general language abilities. The NCS underwent further revisions and the new editions were officially promulgated in 2017 (for compulsory education) and 2022 (for general high school). Similar to the previous editions, the newly-published editions advocate a bringing together of formative and summative assessments in educational assessment, with more emphasis placed on the formative element.

In 2014, the State Council of PRC issued a document entitled *The Implementation Opinions of the State Council on Deepening the Reform of the Examination and Enrollment System*,① requiring the establishment of a comprehensive testing and assessment system of foreign language proficiency. This new assessment and examination system consists of five major components, two of which are the development of *China's Standards of English Language Ability* (the CSE) and the step-by-step establishment of a national educational assessment system bringing together summative and formative assessment.

The CSE was released in February 2018 and put into effect in June of the same year. It defines in a highly generalized way the English language ability of Chinese learners and users in three stages (elementary, intermediate, and advanced), each of which is further divided into three levels. The CSE provides an articulated national standard for EFL teaching and learning at different levels of education and serves as a conceptual framework and guideline for assessment for all language learners (J. D. Liu, 2018). The CSE can be used by EFL teachers as a frame of reference to design assessment activities that are aligned to the curriculum and appropriate for students to better inform instruction.

① The Implementation Opinions of the State Council on Deepening the Reform of the Examination and Enrollment System [National Development Document No. 35(2014)].

On October 13, 2020, the Central Committee and the State Council printed and distributed *The Overall Plan for Deepening the Educational Evaluation Reform in the New Era*,① which stipulates that various assessment methods should be used to cater to the needs of different students at different levels of study and in different types of education. The types of assessment needed include summative assessment, formative assessment, value-added assessment, and comprehensive assessment. This continuation of assessment reform in China is mainly a response to a growing tendency to devolve responsibility for assessment to classroom teachers (e. g. Cumming & Maxwell, 2004; Davison & Leung, 2009) and a global recognition of the centrality of assessment in teaching and learning since the publication of Black and Wiliam's (1998) seminal work. This reform can be characterized as a recurrent attempt to promote a more "emancipatory education" (Flórez Petour, 2014), where the primary objective is learning and the holistic development of students.

To sum up, EFL teachers are called, across policy and curriculum documents, to conduct assessment practices to monitor, support, and report student learning. It has been more than two decades since China first sought to involve teachers in the delivery of a formative assessment policy. Yet, formative assessment remains to be a call rather than actual practice for many language teachers. This provides a new context for us to examine LAL of EFL teachers. What competencies do EFL teachers need to possess in order to implement assessment practices in a responsible and professional manner? What instrument can we use to measure the current LAL levels of this teacher population? And to what extent are they competent in language assessments? These questions require research to address not just the

---

① The Central Committee of the Communist Party of China and the State Council issued "The Overall Plan for Deepening the Educational Evaluation Reform in the New Era"—Government Portal of the Ministry of Education of the People's Republic of China http://www. moe. gov. cn/jyb_xxgk/moe_ 1777/moe_1778/202010/t20201013_494381. html.

theoretical components of LAL required of Chinese EFL teachers, but also to develop a reliable and valid instrument appropriate for the target language teachers. A review of existent assessment literature reveals that there is a scarcity of research in the Chinese educational setting. The current research aims to address these areas of concern.

1.3 Research Rationale

Assessment has been recognized as a dominant aspect of contemporary teaching and learning. Prominent teaching-learning models require that teachers seek information of student mastery of and progress towards desired learning goals to inform their instructional decisions, grading and reporting practices. Danielson's framework for teaching (2013), for instance, expects proficient teachers to be skilled in designing student assessment, using assessment in instruction, and identifying high-quality sources of data for monitoring student growth. Marzano's teacher evaluation model (2013) examines how teachers use assessment to track student progress and document the effectiveness of a particular lesson. The association between instruction and assessment requires that the assessment process be based on the teaching materials being used in class and that classroom teachers have their instruction fine-tuned to students' needs (Poehner, 2008). Hence, teachers need to take a more active role in classroom assessment practices where they have the freedom and capacity to select the right assessment tools and methods that are aligned with the course learning objectives and outcomes.

The success of classroom assessment is closely related to the manner and technique in which it is delivered to learners. Yet, more is dependent upon the objectives of assessment and the teacher assessor. The situation becomes more complex when it comes to language teaching and learning in that language assessment is required to measure the related elements in flux

(Hidri, 2021). This sheds light on the significance of addressing the issues of LAL among EFL programs.

As "a potentially subordinate or overlapping category" to AL (Taylor, 2013, p. 405), LAL is deemed to have multiple dimensions and progressive stages (Pill & Harding, 2013; Taylor, 2013). Researchers have different conceptualizations of LAL, yet there is no agreement upon what specific expertise is included in LAL (Inbar-Lourie, 2013). There is thus a need to explore a body of assessment knowledge and skills Chinese EFL teachers need to possess to be effective in language assessments. This will serve as a good departure for developing an LAL measuring instrument for research and teacher development in assessment.

Researchers have developed several instruments to examine language teachers' LAL, yet most of these instruments target language teachers' general assessment literacy without incorporating the unique characteristics of language assessments. For those few instruments which examine EFL teachers' LAL (e. g. Fulcher, 2012; Hasselgreen *et al.*, 2004; Kremmel & Harding, 2020; Vogt & Tsagari, 2014), most of them are designed for the western educational contexts and used primarily to elicit language teachers' needs in language testing and assessment training, with an aim to inform the design of new teaching materials and the further development of online resources that could be used to support program delivery. Kremmel and Harding's survey is the first and most comprehensive instrument in assessment literature to investigate the LAL training needs of different stakeholders, including language teachers, language testing/assessment developers, and language testing/assessment researchers. For their focus on identifying language teachers' assessment training needs, these existent instruments are not appropriate for the purpose of the current research.

The instrument employed in Xu and G. T. L. Brown (2017) was an adapted version of Plake *et al.*'s (1993) Teacher Assessment Literacy Questionnaire (TALQ). It targets the LAL of Chinese EFL teachers in a higher education context. In addition, the content of the adapted version is aligned with the original survey (with an addition of three items). As Xu and G. T. L. Brown (2017) argue, the items and the underlying constructs in the revised version may not well represent LAL of Chinese university English teachers. Hence, constructing a measuring instrument to investigate Chinese primary and middle school EFL teachers' LAL levels is an urgent need in this field. Furthermore, compared with an increasing body of research on LAL in western educational contexts (Fulcher, 2012; Hasseslgreen *et al.*, 2004; Vogt & Tsagari, 2014), there is a paucity of research addressing EFL teachers' LAL levels in China. Understanding EFL teachers' current competence in language assessment is a good departure for promoting both LAL research and teacher development in assessment.

1.4 Statement of the Research Questions

The significant policy development in China toward standards-based education has resulted in a call for increasing assessment practices within schools and contributed to a greater complexity in the variety of assessments teachers are expected to conduct. Assessment is context-dependent. The competence required for effective language assessments is dependent on a plethora of factors, and the educational setting is an important one. In China, English is learned as a foreign language, and the classroom is the major locus of language learning. Students learn the language mainly via the textbooks (and regrettably, the materials used in many of the textbooks are not quite relevant to students' life), and they seldom have opportunities to learn and use the language after class. The primary purpose that students learn the language is to pass the examinations, not for communication in real life. These factors result in many students' lack of motivation in EFL learning, which, in turn, leads to low efficiency in foreign language learning. To develop and maintain students' interest, EFL teachers need to cater to their affective characteristics and give them a sense of progression. These characteristics of foreign language teaching and learning in China warrant that Chinese EFL teachers need somewhat different competence in language assessment than those language teachers in a context where English is learned as a second language. In the meantime, existent LAL models/profiles are based on western educational settings where English is learned as a second language. They are thus not appropriate for the Chinese educational setting. The current research aims to address these areas of concern and answer the following research questions:

RQ1: What assessment knowledge and skills do Chinese EFL teachers need to possess to assess students' language learning effectively?

RQ2: What instrument can we use to assess Chinese EFL teachers' LAL levels?

RQ3: What are Chinese EFL teachers' current LAL levels?

(1) What is Chinese EFL teachers' overall literacy in language assessment and their expertise in each of the LAL dimensions?

(2) To what extent and in what ways are EFL teachers' demographic characteristics (i. e. grade levels of teaching, assessment training, and the institutional context) related to their different competences in identified LAL dimensions?

1.5 Structure of the Book

This book consists of eight chapters. The first chapter is a general introduction to the current study, including the background, research context, rationale, and the research questions to be addressed.

The second chapter is an extensive review of relevant literature. Research studies in AL in general education were first reviewed with a focus on AL conceptualizations, teachers' conceptions of assessment, contextual considerations of AL, and AL measures. The second part of this chapter is concerned with LAL research studies, focusing upon competing understandings of the LAL construct, studies related to language teachers' beliefs and assessment practices, how to measure LAL, and EFL teachers' professional development in LAL.

Chapter Three is a general introduction to the methodology of the current research. It outlines the design of the research in each stage and gives a brief introduction to the participants, which is followed by an account of how the data were collected and analyzed.

Chapter Four provides a detailed account of how the LAL construct was conceptualized for Chinese EFL teachers based on literature review and analysis of standards documents (professional standards for teachers and prominent assessment standards). This chapter also describes how feedback from domain experts and experienced EFL teachers was sought for the validity of the component structure of the LAL model and how feedback from the experts informed subsequent revisions. The chapter ends with an elucidation of the nature and range of the contents of the constructs in the component structure of the model.

Chapter Five reports the construction of an LAL measuring instrument in line with the LAL model. Opinions were sought from domain experts and the instrument was piloted in two stages. Feedback from these sources brought about many suggestions for revision, and the final item pool was determined. For a clear picture of the questionnaire, the sources, different types of items, and the layout of the questionnaire were specified. In the meantime, empirical evidence was gathered to show construct validity of the questionnaire.

Chapter Six seeks to examine EFL teachers' competence in language assessment. It provides descriptive statistics of EFL teachers' overall LAL levels as well as their competence in different dimensions. Parametric tests were performed to examine how demographic factors were related to teachers' expertise in assessment.

Chapter Seven discusses the research findings and their implications for theory, policy, and practice. Chapter Eight brings the book to a natural conclusion by summarizing the major findings, pointing out the limitations of the current research, and suggesting areas for further study.

CHAPTER TWO
LITERATURE REVIEW

This chapter gives a comprehensive review of relevant studies. AL literature was first reviewed to synthesize the common-core assessment knowledge and skills in general education and the implications they hold for LAL. Then, LAL studies were reviewed with a focus on the elements vital for conducting language assessment in educational settings. To identify relevant studies, we employed a criteria-based scoping review (Arksey & O'Malley, 2005; Xu & G. T. L. Brown, 2016) to create an overview of a diverse body of work. The search included peer-reviewed journal articles, academic books and chapters, unpublished dissertations, and conference papers. All the searches were performed in CALIS, Taylor and Francis Online, Academic Search Premier, ERIC, and Google Scholar. The time span was set from 1990 to 2022 since the first document about teachers' assessment competence appeared in 1990. The search terms include language assessment literacy, assessment literacy, assessment competence, classroom assessment competence, and assessment expertise.

2.1 Assessment Literacy

The concept "literacy", originally used to mean being able to read or write, has been expanded in meaning in the past two decades to refer to the condition or quality of being knowledgeable in a particular subject or field.

Multiplication of literacies has emerged in public and academic discourse in recent years (Taylor, 2013), and one such term is "assessment literacy" (AL) in the community of general education measurement.

The current trends of teacher and school accountability for student learning require that teachers and administrators be literate in assessment to make appropriate interpretations of and decisions about assessment data (Popham, 2008; Stiggins & Chappuis, 2005). AL has become increasingly important and it is "placed at the heart of the success of educational assessment and even the overall quality of education" (Xu & G. T. L. Brown, 2016, p. 134). Due to a growing recognition of the importance of teachers' AL, there is an emerging interest in AL studies, revolving around the LAL construct, teachers' conceptions of assessment, contextual considerations of AL, and AL measures.

2.1.1 The AL construct

The complex construct of AL has evoked a growing body of research in the past three decades. This subsection gives an account of how this construct is conceptualized in the general education community.

2.1.1.1 Definitions of AL

Stiggins (1991) coined the term "assessment literacy" to refer to the knowledge about educational assessment and the skills required to apply that knowledge to measure student learning. A lack of AL could "cripple the quality of education" (Popham, 2009, p. 4). Yet, there is a lack of agreement upon what AL might comprise, despite an increasing diversity of approaches recommended to encourage its development (e. g. Walters, 2010), as evidenced in the competing definitions in the literature.

Sadler (1998) summarizes six characteristics of assessment competent teachers: (1) superior knowledge about curriculum-related content to be learned; (2) knowledge about learners and learning and a desire to help students develop, improve, and do better; (3) skills in selecting and creating assessment tasks; (4) knowledge of criteria and standards appropriate to assessment tasks; (5) evaluative skills and expertise in the analysis and use of assessment evidence; and (6) expertise in giving appropriate and targeted feedback. Mertler (2003) states that assessment literate educators recognize sound assessment, evaluation, and communication practices. They understand which assessment methods to use to gather dependable information about student achievement, communicate assessment results effectively, whether using report card grades, test scores, portfolios, or conferences. They can use assessment to maximize student motivation and learning by involving students as full partners in assessment, record keeping, and communication.

Popham (2011a) defines AL broadly as "an individual's understandings of the fundamental assessment concepts and procedures deemed likely to influence educational decisions" (p. 267). This definition implies that an assessment literate teacher has the know-how and understanding of assessment in order to assess their students effectively and maximize their learning. Vogt and Tsagari (2014) define AL as "the ability to design, develop, and critically evaluate tests and other assessment procedures, as well as the ability to monitor, evaluate, grade, and score assessments on the basis of theoretical knowledge"(p. 377). Looney et al. (2017) define AL as "teacher capabilities to plan and implement quality assessment tasks, to interpret evidence and outcomes appropriate to the assessment purpose and type, and to engage students themselves as active participants in assessment of their own learning" (p. 2).

Willis et al. (2013) argue that AL is a dynamic, context-dependent social practice that involves teachers articulating and negotiating classroom and cultural knowledge with one another and with learners in the initiation, development, and practice of assessment to achieve the learning. Gareis and Grant (2015b) view AL as a professional competency that every teacher should be required to develop and demonstrate for purposes of licensure. They define AL as the ability to make and use valid and reliable assessments as a classroom teacher to facilitate and communicate student learning.

As can be seen from the various conceptualizations above, earlier definitions of AL are mainly concerned with teacher assessment, and they revolve around the practical aspects of assessment, such as skills, strategies, or the various activities a teacher needs to conduct (Gotch & French, 2014; Schafer & Lissitz, 1987). Some notions of AL also emphasize measurement qualities. With a paradigm shift from assessment of learning to assessment for learning (Andrade, 2013; Andrade & Heritage, 2018; Stiggins, 2010; Wiliam, 2010) and a social turn of language testing (McNamara & Roever, 2006), there is a multitude of factors that shape teachers' assessment practices and a dramatic shift in the way AL is conceived. AL has been characterized by two important features, i. e. the use of assessment to facilitate learning and the context-dependent nature of assessment activities.

2. 1. 1. 2 Components of AL

The definitions above are broad conceptualizations of AL and are not explicit in terms of the specific components. Some research organizations (e. g. AFT, NCME, & NEA) and researchers delineate the various components of assessment that classroom teachers need to be skilled in (e. g. Brookhart, 2011; Pastore & Andrade, 2019; Stiggins, 2010; Stiggins et al., 2004; Stiggins & DuFour, 2009; Xu & G. T. L. Brown, 2016).

In 1990, the American Federation of Teachers, National Council on Measurement in Education, and National Education Association (AFT, NCME, & NEA) jointly developed the *Standards for Teacher Competence in Educational Assessment of Students* (the 1990 Standards for short), which includes seven standards as follows.

(1) Teachers should be skilled in choosing assessment methods appropriate for instructional decisions;

(2) Teachers should be skilled in developing assessment methods appropriate for instructional decisions;

(3) Teachers should be skilled in administering, scoring, and interpreting the results of both externally produced and teacher-produced assessment methods;

(4) Teachers should be skilled in using assessment results when making decisions about individual students, planning teaching, developing curriculum, and school improvement;

(5) Teachers should be skilled in developing valid pupil grading procedures that use pupil assessments;

(6) Teachers should be skilled in communicating assessment results to students, parents, other lay audiences, and other educators; and

(7) Teachers should be skilled in recognizing unethical, illegal, and otherwise inappropriate assessment methods and uses of assessment information.

The 1990 Standards is the first document that specifies the general knowledge and skills teachers need to possess in order to assess students' learning. It made a considerable contribution to teacher education programs (Airasian & Russell, 2007; Mertler, 2003; Miller *et al.*, 2009; Nitko & Brookhart, 2007) and the educational measurement community (Mertler, 2003; Mertler & Campbell, 2005; O'Sullivan & Johnson, 1993; Plake *et al.*, 1993). Though developed for the American educational context, these standards have been referenced in investigations of teachers' AL development across educational contexts. Many studies, based on the 1990 Standards, have been conducted to investigate the knowledge base of AL in different subject areas (e. g. science and language) (Abell & Siegel, 2011; Gottheiner & Siegel, 2012; Inbar-Lourie, 2008a; Scarino, 2013; Vogt & Tsagari, 2014), for different assessment purposes (learning vs.

accountability) (Willis *et al.*, 2013), and with different stakeholders (i. e. teachers, students, and administrators) (e. g. Plake *et al.*, 1993; Taylor, 2013).

The 1990 Standards continues to be relevant to the assessment expectations of teachers today, but the set of knowledge and skills described has more relevance to summative assessment and becomes outdated in today's accountability and standards-based educational context. For teachers, AL is mainly concerned with the ability to conduct classroom assessments that provide reliable information about student learning towards learning targets and the capacity to make data-driven decisions about teaching and learning. Recent studies have proposed updated lists of the knowledge base, calling for an inclusion of capabilities based upon recent developments in assessment policy and practice, i. e. formative assessment and accountability contexts (Brookhart, 2011; Chappuis, 2015; McMillan, 2000; Stiggins, 2010).

Popham (2018) conceptualizes AL as six high-priority concepts (validity, reliability, and fairness) and procedures (score reports, formative assessments, and measuring affect). Popham's AL framework is marked by a balance between summative and formative assessments. It draws most of the assessment concepts and procedures from standards for educational assessment (e. g. the 1990 Standards). Yet, this model is innovative for an expansion of knowledge needed by teachers, that is, the inclusion of understanding students' affect in assessment.

With growing popularity of formative assessment in the classroom, Stiggins (2008, 2009, 2010) proposes a framework of competence in quality assessment, which includes five keys that classroom teachers need to bear in mind when conducting classroom assessment: clear purposes, clear targets, sound assessment design, effective communication, and student involvement. Different from the 1990 Standards, Stiggins' framework incorporates formative assessment and student involvement in assessment and provides a good representation of classroom assessment competencies for teachers in today's standards-based education context. Nevertheless, this framework lacks the details necessary to provide explicit guidance for teachers, teacher educators, and measurement specialists (Brookhart, 2011). Additionally, the AL components are restricted to the domain of educational assessment in a narrow sense. Little attention is given to other factors that may mediate teachers' AL and assessment practice.

Willis *et al.* (2013) employ a Bernsteinian approach to discussing the components of AL in terms of vertical and horizontal assessment discourse. AL in a horizontal discourse refers to critical inquiries into assessment processes and practices in actual contexts (Wyatt-Smith & Gunn, 2009), while AL in a vertical structure focuses on the knowledge required to identify students' misconceptions and gaps in learning, and the capabilities to diagnose students' needs and position them on a developmental continuum (Griffin *et al.*, 2005; quoted from Willis *et al.*, 2013). Willis *et al.* (2013) define AL as "a dynamic, context-dependent social practice that involves teachers articulating and negotiating classroom and cultural knowledge with one another and with learners in the initiation, development, and practice of assessment to achieve the learning goals of students" (p. 242). Willis *et al.*'s (2013) conceptualization highlights a dynamic and negotiated concept. AL is not taken as a singular set of capabilities but as a competence that is situated, socially and culturally shaped. This sociocultural view of AL is congruent with a sociocultural perspective on learning (DeLuca *et al.*, 2016a; Xu & G. T. L. Brown, 2016), and enables teachers to respond to assessments based on their constructed understanding of assessment as socially situated within their teaching context (DeLuca *et al.*, 2016a).

Xu and G. T. L. Brown (2016) conceptualize AL by connecting fields of educational assessment and teacher education, and construct a new conceptual framework of teacher assessment literacy in practice (TALiP).

This process-oriented, hierarchical model includes six components: knowledge base, teacher conceptions of assessment, institutional and socio-cultural contexts, teacher assessment literacy in practice, teacher learning, and teacher identity (re)construction as assessor. TALiP is not static but "constantly negotiated between teachers' conceptions of assessment and the macro socio-cultural, micro institutional contexts, and expected knowledge base" (Xu & G. T. L. Brown, 2016, p. 157), reflecting compromises among tensions.

Building on this framework, Xu and G. T. L. Brown (2016) propose a working definition of TALiP, which consists of three different levels of mastery. The first is a basic understanding of assessment knowledge, mainly including the fundamental principles of the "what", "why", and "how" of assessment. The second level is an internalized set of understanding and appreciation of the interconnectedness of assessment, teaching, and learning, which is more of a personal nature. The third is a self-directed awareness of assessment processes and one's own identity as an assessor. Such awareness allows teachers to accommodate and translate assessment policies and principles into classroom practices.

Xu and G. T. L. Brown's framework shows that AL is culturally situated and contextually sensitive, and its development is a systematic enterprise with joint efforts from appropriate stakeholders. This model is innovative by moving the assessment field beyond a focus on the knowledge base to a consideration of a contextualized, dynamic, and evolving system in which teachers make compromises among competing tensions. Teachers' pedagogical content knowledge (PCK) and curriculum-related knowledge are recognized as important elements of teachers' assessment knowledge base. This adds a content specific aspect to assessment competence. Xu and G. T. L. Brown (2016) also recognize the significance of reconstruction of teachers' identity as assessors in the development of AL. A plethora of factors, such as conceptions of assessment, beliefs, experiences, and feelings, affect the way teachers conceptualize their role in assessment, and more research is needed in this area (Looney *et al.*, 2017).

Herppich *et al.* (2018) conceptualize assessment competence as context-specific, learnable cognitive dispositions that are needed to successfully cope with specific assessment situations. They propose a conceptual model of teacher assessment competence with integration of studies of assessment processes, practices, and products. This model is framed in two sub-models. The structural sub-model serves to explicate how the elements of the model link with each other, and the process sub-model shows how (assessment) competence-related cognitive judgment processes and assessment practices interact to affect assessment products. This conceptualization of assessment competence values teachers' knowledge, beliefs, and motivations (e. g. Deluca *et al.*, 2016b; Xu & G. T. L. Brown, 2016) and recognizes variations in assessment performance in different contexts (see Willis *et al.*, 2013; Xu & G. T. L. Brown, 2016). The model also assumes assessment competence to be learnable and measurable in classes of professional situations (Kaiser *et al.*, 2017; Koeppen *et al.*, 2008). This assumption has implications for promoting teacher AL that draws upon inherent dispositions and processes with an equivalent focus on the context-dependence of assessments (Herppich *et al.*, 2018; Kaiser *et al.*, 2017). It also allows for cognitively based explanations of teachers' assessment practices via reliable and valid measurements in different situations.

Pastore and Andrade (2019) take a holistic and adaptive perspective on competencies to identify the qualities of an assessment literate teacher in today's educational context. Their model includes three inter-related but differently prioritized dimensions: conceptual, praxeological, and socio-emotional. The conceptual knowledge dimension mainly refers to the what, why, and how of assessment as well as data analysis and communication of assessment results. The praxeological dimension refers to the various processes of assessment practices, most of which are identified in previous AL models. However, this dimension places more emphasis on formative assessment than on summative assessment, for its inclusion of defining learning targets and assessment criteria, making use of assessment results to facilitate learning, and providing feedback. The socio-emotional dimension mainly refers to teachers' awareness of their identity as assessor, ethics in assessment, and emotional dynamics of students. In this model, AL is defined not just in terms of its conceptual and practical aspects but also in relation to the emotional and social aspects, indicative of recent attempts to focus on teachers' dispositions, their identity as assessors, and the ethical aspects of classroom assessment (Adie, 2013; Looney *et al.*, 2017). The dynamic nature of this model offers an explanation to the constant question of why teacher education and theory alone are not effective in promoting teachers' AL. It also merits our attention that the construction of Pastore and Andrade's (2019) model undergoes iterative inquiries from a considerable number of experts in the assessment community, and the input and support from these scholars lend credence to its validity.

The competing definitions and models of teacher AL discussed above indicate that conceptualizations of the types of knowledge and skills underpinning AL have been influenced by sociocultural theories of teaching and learning and the growing recognition of the social role of assessment in education (Broadfoot, 1996, 2005; Inbar-Lourie, 2008a). AL has evolved from a single-dimension concept of monitoring, recording, improving, and reporting student learning into a multidimensional construct. Research studies of teacher assessment literacy provide important insights into the types of knowledge and skills that are relevant to the educational assessment of students (e. g. Brookhart, 2011; DeLuca *et al.*, 2016a; Stiggins, 2008, 2009, 2010; Popham, 2009), inform us how teachers' dispositions, such as their conceptions of assessments and affect, might influence their translation of assessment theory into practices (e. g. Brookhart, 2011; Herppich *et al.*, 2018; Pastore & Andrade, 2019; Xu & G. T. L. Brown, 2016). These studies also emphasize the relevance of context for teachers' professional actions, viewing assessment as situation-dependent practice that is culturally and socially shaped (DeLuca *et al.*, 2016a; Herppich *et al.*, 2018; Willis *et al.*, 2013; Xu & G. T. L. Brown, 2016).

2.1.2 Teachers' conceptions of assessment

The call in recent years to integrate assessment with instruction (Black & Wiliam, 1998) and a growing recognition of the centrality of classroom assessment in the learning process have brought about an increased interest in teachers' perceptions of assessment practices. Conceptions of assessment (CoA) refers to the attitudes, perceptions, dispositions, etc. that suggest teachers' beliefs about the nature and purpose of assessment. The research interest in teachers' CoA is relatively recent (Barnes *et al.*, 2017; G. T. L. Brown, 2004, 2006, 2008; Harris & Brown, 2009). G. T. L. Brown (2008) states that teachers' CoA may be categorized into four major purposes: informing educational improvement, evaluating schools and teachers, evaluating students, and irrelevance. Improvement means that teachers and students make evidence-based decisions about student learning to bridge the gap between students' current learning and learning goals. Evaluation focuses on comparing student performance against preset standards, assigning scores, and certifying competence. School evaluation is concerned with the use of assessment results to determine the performance of teachers and schools. Irrelevance is taken to mean either considering assessment as irrelevant to learning or deeming it negative for students.

Later research, however, identifies different models of CoA in teachers. Remesal (2007, 2009, 2011) focuses on teachers' understandings of assessment in terms of four dimensions: teaching, learning, accreditation of learning, and accountability. The four dimensions are interwoven and represent a global conception of the functions of assessment: pedagogical regulation and societal accreditation. Xu and G. T. L. Brown (2016) identify two dimensions of CoA—cognitive and affective. The cognitive dimension is related to teacher belief systems when evaluating students' performance, whereas the affective dimension denotes teacher emotion towards assessment. CoA functions as a potent mediator of assessment planning and practice within contextual tensions. The strong accountability function of assessment renders it difficult to implement formative assessment reform, and some teachers take formative assessment as "something extra" rather than an essential part of instruction (Neesom, 2000).

G. T. L. Brown and Gao (2015) identify a different profile of CoA among Chinese teachers. Through a synthesis of eight interview and survey studies with a diverse sample of participant teachers, Brown and Gao find that Chinese teachers have different conceptions of the nature and purpose of assessment, including facilitation and diagnosis, ability development, personal quality, institutional targets, management and inspection, and negativity (ranging from positively regarded ideas to negative conceptualization). The conceptions of improvement, accountability, and irrelevance are identified with teachers in a western context, but conceptions like ability development and personal quality are specific to a Chinese educational context, suggesting a cultural and policy impact on teachers' CoA.

CoA is also dynamic, changing in response to teachers' learning experience (G. T. L. Brown, 2011b; G. T. L. Brown & Remesal, 2012; Harrison, 2005; C. Lee & Wiliam, 2005; L. Lin et al., 2021), assessment practice (G. T. L. Brown, 2011a; Xu & L. Y. He, 2019), context, and career stage (G. T. L. Brown, 2004). G. T. L. Brown (2011b) finds prospective teachers have different CoAs from practicing teachers though they have some shared understandings of assessment, like negativity of assessment and assessment for student accountability. G. T. L. Brown and Remesal (2012) made a cultural comparison of CoA of prospective and practising teachers in New Zealand and Spain. They obtained similar research findings with G. T. L. Brown (2011b), but noticed a difference in the response between the two participant samples due to cultural and societal priorities. The context-dependent nature of CoA is also echoed in L. Lin *et al.* (2021). L. Lin *et al.* (2021) utilized G. T. L. Brown's (2006) TCoA-IIIA questionnaire as an instrument to investigate CoA held by pre-service teachers in China's second language education. Different from G. T. L. Brown's study, they found eight distinct first-order factors and different profiles of CoA among these pre-service teachers (improvement-oriented, balanced, and negative). Xu and L. Y. He (2019) find Chinese pre-service teachers undergo a radical shift in their understanding of assessment. Before practicum, most of the pre-service teachers conceived assessment as performing two functions: academic achievement and moral character development. However, after a period of teaching practice, they came to recognize the multiple purposes of assessment, constructs in evaluation criteria, teacher feedback, concerns of fairness in classroom assessment, and students' involvement in assessment. This change in conception was the result of an interaction of personal, experiential, and contextual factors.

A growing body of evidence suggests that the assessment process and outcomes may be affected by teachers' CoA (e. g. G. T. L. Brown, 2008; Leung, 2004; Pajares, 1992). Teachers' beliefs about assessment purposes are connected to their beliefs about teaching, learning, and curriculum, and the endorsement of varied assessment purposes predicts different kinds of assessment practices on the part of teachers (G. T. L. Brown, 2008). Quilter and Chester (1998) found that in-service teachers who were positive about standardized testing were more likely to see less value in alternative forms of assessment, while those who were more positive about classroom assessment tended to be more accepting of alternative forms of assessment.

Deneen and G. T. L. Brown (2016) argue that teachers' AL and CoA are two equally important factors that can affect teachers' assessment practices. Shepard (2006) highlights the power of conceptions and the importance of taking them into account in understanding how teachers implement classroom assessment. Teachers' conceptions of assessment purposes affect, to a large extent, assessment practices at all educational levels (Brookhart, 2011; Deneen & G. T. L. Brown, 2016; Fulmer *et al.*, 2015; Vandeyar & Killen, 2007). Positive CoA is shown to be connected with beneficial assessment practices, while negative conceptions may cause teachers to resist or subvert innovative changes in assessment policies and intended practices (G. T. L. Brown, 2008; Deneen & Boud, 2014; Remesal, 2007). Teachers who hold that assessment can be used to facilitate learning will conduct formative assessment practices on a regular basis. Czerniak and Lumpe (1996) suggest that teacher conceptions about science education reform are the best predictor of classroom implementation of assessment since teachers with constructivist beliefs have a richer repertoire of assessment strategies to induce students' learning. However, teachers may have inconsistent understandings of the functions of assessments in instructional decision-making (Wininger & Norman, 2005).

Nevertheless, some researchers have identified a gap between teachers' reported CoA and assessment practices (Bol & Strage, 1996; Morrison & Lederman, 2003). Though some teachers value classroom assessment for its potentials for facilitating explicit learning and promoting learning autonomy, they are more involved in practices that support a performance orientation in students (Barnes *et al.*, 2017). Remesal's (2011) analysis of teacher interviews suggests that teachers' CoA may consist of different and sometimes contrasting beliefs about the various roles of assessment. Thus, it is important for researchers and teacher educators to consider different assessment beliefs and not to take for granted that the beliefs about what to assess are consistent with beliefs about the tasks/activities used to assess.

If a teacher's CoA contradicts with the current views of effective assessment practices, those beliefs would hinder efforts to restructure classroom assessment.

Beyond the diversity of studies of CoA held by teachers, another line of enquiry is the factors that influence these types of conceptions. Studies have shown that various factors can influence teachers' CoA, like teachers' past experiences with educational assessment (Pajares, 1992; Quilter & Gallini, 2000), the educational system where teachers work, understanding of the subject area (Vandeyar & Killen, 2007), teachers' beliefs about students' abilities, the community expectations (Bright & Joyner, 1998), etc. Assessment training/education is another important factor to consider in studies of teachers' CoA. Studies have indicated that assessment education has little influence on teachers' CoA, which remains largely unchanged and negative (Deneen & G. T. L. Brown, 2011, 2016). Some other research has suggested that teachers' CoA may change in response to specific experiences in their career, but the extent of change is affected by several factors, from the target beliefs through the length and nature of the experience to individual and contextual factors (Levy-Vered & Alhija, 2015).

As shown above, research into teachers' CoA is essential for an understanding of the complex nature of teachers' assessment practices. Positive CoA can exert a direct positive influence on AL (Levy-Vered & Alhija, 2015), and recent AL models incorporate CoA as an essential component (e. g. DeLuca et al., 2016b; Xu & G. T. L. Brown, 2016). CoA has become an important component in examining teacher AL/LAL.

2.1.3 Contextual considerations of AL

AL is a dynamic, multi-dimensional construct with various factors coming into play in its manifestation. Yet, there is insufficient empirical research on how contextual factors affect teacher AL. Inferences from empirical studies of teacher AL and classroom assessment practices suggest that factors at different levels (national, aggregate, and individual) influence AL in various ways (Xu & G. T. L. Brown, 2016). At the national level, curriculum standards (Fenwick, 2017), teacher accreditation requirements (Greenberg & Walsh, 2012; Tierney, 2006), and high-stakes large-scale tests (Collins *et al.*, 2010; Gu, 2014) affect teachers' AL by shaping pre-service education and professional development activities and teacher autonomy (Forsberg & Wermke, 2012). At the aggregate level, factors such as power relations in the workplace, teaching environment, and students' learning needs help shape teachers' AL (Tierney, 2006; Willis *et al.*, 2013; Xu & Y. C. Liu, 2009). At the personal level, teachers' awareness of classroom assessment, their identity as assessors, and latent personality traits also come into play (Adie, 2013; DeLuca *et al.*, 2019a; Looney *et al.*, 2017; Scarino, 2013). These factors were addressed separately in empirical research, but how they interrelate with each other and how they, when combined together, influence AL development and assessment practice remain to be explored (Xu & G. T. L. Brown, 2016).

Assessment is not a value-free concept (Goldstein, 1991; Taylor, 2013). Assessment tasks are embedded in social and political contexts. People of different social classes, ethnicity, age, or gender will respond differently to the tasks (Maclellan, 2004). Some researchers employ an integrated approach to AL and place emphasis on teachers as professionals whose AL is dependent on the context rather than on the understanding of assessment principles (Frey & Fisher, 2009). In line with sociocultural theories of learning, AL is conceptualized as context-responsive and culturally shaped practices that teachers negotiate with their students in learning communities (Willis *et al.*, 2013), and professional judgement of student learning is perceived as an individual cognitive act and a socially situated practice (Allal, 2013). With this contextualized view, teacher AL becomes a joint enterprise requiring support from different stakeholder groups, such as policy makers, school administrators, teacher educators, students, and even the general public (Allal, 2013; Fleer, 2015). Still, teachers remain to be the main drivers of their AL development. They need to make full use of classroom assessment practices to gain a better understanding of assessment processes (Borko *et al.*, 1997; Buck & Trauth-Nare, 2009; Gottheiner & Siegel, 2012), engage in conversations and collaboration with colleagues (Engelsen & Smith, 2014; Wyatt-Smith *et al.*, 2010), and participate in assessment training provided by professional development programs (Frey & Fisher, 2009; Willis *et al.*, 2013). Teachers also need to be aware of their CoA (Leung, 2014), since it could be a facilitator or an inhibitor to their AL development (Borko *et al.*, 1997; Siegel & Wissehr, 2011).

These studies of a contextualized conception of AL show that teachers are placed in complex contexts to make professional decisions about assessment in response to various factors that may facilitate or inhibit their practices (Xu & Brown, 2016). They draw upon a multitude of sources of knowledge and evidence when making decisions (Cooksey *et al.*, 2007; Davison, 2004), ranging from personal knowledge of students, the curriculum and teaching contexts, to prior assessment experience (as a student) and individual tacit knowledge of standards for judgement purposes (Connolly *et al.*, 2012). Teacher AL is a highly complex, dynamic, and ongoing process, built on past experiences, present actions, and future plans (Xu & Y. C. Liu, 2009). Situating teachers' decision-making and action-taking processes amidst the multitude of factors at play in specific contexts is essential to understanding and developing teacher AL (Xu & Brown, 2016).

2.1.4 AL measures

With a wide recognition of the importance of AL for teachers, there is a growing body of research into teachers' AL levels over the past two or three decades. Various instruments have been constructed to measure and track pre-service and in-service teachers' AL in an effort to support their classroom assessment practices. The majority of measures have focused on teachers' levels of assessment knowledge and skills (e. g. O'Sullivan & Johnson, 1993; Plake et al., 1993), or related factors like confidence in assessment (e. g. DeLuca et al., 2016b; Volante & Fazio, 2007) and perceptions of assessment purposes (e. g. G. T. L. Brown, 2004). Recent years also witness an evolving area of research into teachers' negotiated practices within and across cultural contexts (e. g. Cowie & Carr, 2004; DeLuca et al., 2019b; Lopez & Pasquini, 2017). A comprehensive review of all the studies is beyond the scope of this book, and the following is mainly concerned with quantitative measures used to examine teachers' assessment knowledge and skills.

Many of the AL measures identified in the research take the form of objective tests (e. g. D. L. Lin, 2016; Mertler, 2003; O'Sullivan & Johnson, 1993; Plake et al., 1993; T. H. Wang et al., 2008). Plake et al. (1993) was the first study to address the AL levels of teachers and administrators and received considerable attention in the measurement community. They constructed Teacher Competencies Assessment Questionnaire (TCAQ) to examine assessment competence of teachers and administrators in the United States. This instrument included 35 items, with five multiple-choice items targeting each standard of the 1990 Standards. The results showed that teachers had insufficient understanding and use of assessments as indicated by an average of 23 items answered correctly. These participant teachers also demonstrated different levels of competence in different standards. Specifically, they were more competent in choosing and developing assessment methods, administering, and scoring, but lacked knowledge and skills in interpreting, integrating, and communicating assessment results.

TCAQ was used and/or adapted in many later studies (e. g. Campbell et al., 2002; Mertler, 2003; O'Sullivan & Johnson, 1993; Xu & Brown, 2017). O'Sullivan and Johnson (1993) used TCAQ to determine the AL of graduate students enrolled in a performance-based measurement course which was aligned with the 1990 Standards. The students' different performances on TACQ before and after instruction showed that they had improved literacy in assessment. Campbell *et al.* (2002) used a revised version of this instrument to measure the AL levels of undergraduate students enrolled in a pre-service measurement course and identified a similar trend with Plake *et al.* (1993). Mertler (2003) also got similar research results when he administered the TCAQ to pre- and in-service teachers. Mertler and Campbell (2004, 2005) revised TCAQ into the Assessment Literacy Inventory (ALI) by contextualizing the items in scenario-based questions. The ALI consisted of seven scenarios that matched the seven standards in the 1990 Standards. Mertler and Campbell (2004, 2005) administered the ALI to pre-service teachers enrolled in a measurement course to measure their learning in relation to the 1990 Standards. The training proved to be effective for the teachers, as evidenced by the significant differences in ALI scores between the two administrations. Consistent with previous studies, this research found these teachers lacked competence in critical aspects of assessment.

D. H. Zheng (2009) employed a translated, abridged version of TCAQ (with 3 items covering each of the standards in the 1990 Standards) to investigate the AL of teachers in primary and middle schools in an eastern coastal province in China. The study found an even lower level of understanding and use of assessments on the part of these Chinese teachers. As Xu and Brown (2017) argue, it is insufficient to adapt an imported measuring instrument designed in a western educational context three decades ago to measure Chinese teacher AL in the contemporary educational setting. More research is needed to better align the measuring tool with the Chinese assessment contexts.

Some other psychometric instruments take the form of questionnaires to measure teachers' perceived competence in assessment (e. g. DeLuca &

Klinger, 2010; Gotch & French, 2014; Koloi-Keaikitse, 2012; D. L. Lin, 2016; Volante & Fazio, 2007; Xu & Brown, 2017; Z. C. Zhang & Burry-Stock, 2003). Volante and Fazio (2007) employed a survey to examine the AL of primary and junior school teacher candidates from each year of an education program and identified different levels of self-perceived AL across the multiple aspects of classroom assessment. Z. C. Zhang and Burry-Stock (2003) examined 297 teachers' assessment practices and self-perceived assessment skills. The instrument used in the study—Assessment Practices Inventory (Z. C. Zhang & Burry-Stock, 1997)—was developed based on literature on classroom assessment and the 1990 Standards. The results demonstrated that teachers enrolled in measurement training reported enhanced self-perceived assessment skills. Xu and Brown (2017) used an adapted version of TACQ to examine the AL of 891 Chinese University English teachers and found a basic level of competence in these teachers. Meanwhile, they conducted a psychometric properties analysis of the adapted TACQ in the study. The result lends credibility to the validity of only a few items, confirming Fulcher's (2012) skepticism of "little operational structural integrity" (p. 117) with the constructs in the TALQ. D. L. Lin (2016) developed an AL inventory to measure Chinese middle school English teachers' perceived knowledge and skills in assessment and found a moderate level of competence (with an average of 4 out of 6) in the respondent English teachers. However, different from previous studies, the psychometric property of the scale was established with exploratory and confirmatory factor analyses.

Rubrics are a third type of measures used to examine teachers' assessment competence (Campbell & Evans, 2000; Koh, 2011; McMorris & Boothroyd, 1993). Campbell and Evans (2000) used a checklist to analyze 309 assessment plans from 65 pre-service teachers enrolled in a measurement course, and found many of the assessment practices recommended in the coursework were not followed in the pre-service teachers' assessment plans. Sato *et al.* (2008) used a 5-point rubric to examine the extent of use and the quality of formative assessment in National Board participants' classroom practices at different periods over 3 years and observed pronounced changes in these candidates in all the six dimensions of formative assessment. Koh (2011) used a rubric to examine the effects of professional development on teachers' AL and found teachers enrolled in ongoing, sustained professional development gained higher levels of AL than those involved in short-term, one-shot workshops in authentic assessment.

Overall, results from these studies consistently indicate teachers' insufficient AL as required by the 1990 Standards. Gotch and French (2014) conducted a comprehensive review of the AL measures (objective tests, surveys, and rubrics), and found there was little psychometric evidence to support claims about the fundamental aspects of measurement, i. e. test content, internal consistency reliability, score stability, internal structure, and association with other variables. Additionally, these measures were predicated on outdated assessment standards documents (i. e. the 1990 Standards) or literature on fundamental aspects of assessment. Many of them do not consider the relevance and representativeness of content in relation to paradigm shift in the assessment landscape (DeLuca *et al.*, 2016a), which is characterized by educational accountability systems, conceptions of formative assessment (Brookhart, 2011), and an emerging trend of assessment education.

DeLuca *et al.* (2016a) constructed a new AL instrument—Approaches to Classroom Assessment Instrument (ACAI), based on a document analysis of 15 assessment standards documents (1990—2015) from six geographic areas. This new instrument is divided into three parts. The first part, Approaches to Classroom Assessment, includes five scenarios reflective of the contemporary assessment landscape: summative assessment, grading, differentiated assessment, integrated assessment, and standardized assessment. Every scenario covers four multiple-choice items, with each corresponding to one of the four AL themes, i. e. assessment purposes, assessment processes, fairness, and measurement theory. The second part, Confidence in Classroom Assessment, is built on the Classroom Assessment Standards (JCSEE, 2015). It examines teachers' perceived confidence level in relation to each standard on a 5-point Likert scale. The third part, Assessment Education and Support for Teachers, is intended to determine teachers' priorities and preferences in professional assessment learning on a 5-point Likert scale. Unlike previous measures, the ACAI reflects the core aspects of contemporary teacher assessment policy and practices. It serves as a new instrument to lend support to research and professional development in the area of teacher assessment literacy (DeLuca et al., 2016a).

Assessment is viewed as a contextually grounded practice that is socially and culturally shaped, aligned with a sociocultural perspective on learning. New AL measures need to be contextually grounded in line with the assessment policy, priorities, and traditions within the specific context (Xu & Brown, 2017). In the meantime, they need to incorporate differences in educational settings since assessment priorities vary with education levels (ibid) and subject areas.

To sum up, the contextual nature of AL calls for more research into the following areas (Taylor, 2013): (1) defining the AL construct; (2) language and discourse needed when addressing a non-specialist audience; (3) identifying, evaluating, and responding to stakeholder needs in AL; and (4) growth of AL over time. Assessment practice focuses on a specific domain of knowledge. Classroom teachers need to combine their common-core AL with the particular subject content they intend to measure. The next section discusses language assessment literacy (LAL) due to its unique complexities in the assessment of language skills, knowledge, and communicative competence (Harding & Kremmel, 2016; Inbar-Lourie, 2008a; Jeong, 2013; Taylor, 2013).

2.2 Language Assessment Literacy

For language teachers, being assessment competent means possessing a repertoire of assessment knowledge and skills combined with language-specific competencies (Inbar-Lourie, 2008a). This section reviews relevant LAL studies to provide a complete picture of the current status of LAL research, which will have clear pedagogical implications for classroom EFL teachers and teacher educators.

2.2.1 The LAL Construct

Defining LAL is challenging due to its complex nature. Broadly speaking, LAL can be understood as the knowledge and skills required for language teachers (and other stakeholders) to conduct and use language assessments effectively (e. g. Fulcher, 2012; Inbar-Lourie, 2008a). It has been conceptualized differently and competing definitions can be found in the literature.

2. 2. 1. 1 Definitions of LAL

Brindley (2001) was the first language testing professional to research AL, arguing for attention to curriculum-related assessment. He also placed emphasis on the social context of testing and on the need to define and assess language proficiency, construct and use tests and assessments to gauge achievement against a curriculum. More importantly, Brindley (2001) urged assessment educators to recognize the need to develop flexible approaches to assessment practices. These recommendations forecast Davies' (2008) concern for an expansion of the content in traditional books on language testing to incorporate the needs of the new century.

Inbar-Lourie (2008a) adopts an interpretative, constructivist approach to assessment. In this approach, assessment is not value-free (Goldstein, 1991; Taylor, 2013). It is "socially constructed under the influence of dominant epistemological assumptions, educational preconceptions, and social, political, and cultural beliefs" (Inbar-Lourie, 2008a, p. 390). With this socially oriented conception, Inbar-Lourie (2008a) places social context at the heart of assessment and assessment literacy, and explores LAL in terms of three dimensions: the reasoning or rationale for assessment (the "why"), the description of the trait to be assessed (the "what"), and the assessment process (the "how"). Inbar-Lourie calls for the establishment of an assessment culture where people "share epistemological suppositions about the dynamic nature of knowledge" (p. 387). This conceptualization construes language assessment as "a body of knowledge and research grounded in theory and epistemological beliefs, and connected to other bodies of knowledge in education, linguistics, and applied linguistics" (Inbar-Lourie, 2008a, p. 396).

Inbar-Lourie (2013) argues that LAL is a unique complex entity. It shares components with AL in general education but also has its own features. Inbar-Lourie proposes eight ingredients of LAL for language teachers, which are listed as follows:

- Understanding the social role of assessment and the responsibility of the language tester, understanding the political [and] social forces involved, test power, and consequences;
- Knowledge on how to write, administer, and analyze tests, report test results and ensure test quality;
- Understanding of large scale test data;
- Proficiency in language classroom assessment;
- Mastering language acquisition and learning theories and relating to them in the assessment process;
- Matching assessment with language teaching approaches, knowledge about current language teaching approaches and pedagogies;
- Awareness of the dilemmas that underlie assessment, i. e. formative vs. summative, internal vs. external validity, and reliability issues

particularly with reference to authentic language use;

- LAL is individualized, the product of the knowledge, experience, perceptions, and beliefs that language teachers bring to the teaching and assessment process.

(Inbar-Lourie, 2013)

Taylor (2009) defines LAL as language teachers' familiarity with assessment methods and the ability to apply this knowledge in actual assessment practices. Specifically, LAL refers to language teachers' knowledge of and skills in selecting, administering, interpreting, and sharing results of external large-scale tests as well as the expertise in developing, scoring, interpreting, and improving classroom-based assessments.

Fulcher (2012) comes to the most comprehensive working definition of LAL through empirical research investigating the assessment training needs of language teachers, which is as follows.

The knowledge, skills and abilities required to design, develop, maintain or evaluate, large-scale standardized and/or classroom based tests, familiarity with test processes, and awareness of principles and concepts that guide and underpin practice, including ethics and codes of practice. The ability to place knowledge, skills, processes, principles and concepts within wider historical, social, political and philosophical frameworks in order to understand why practices have arisen as they have, and to evaluate the role and impact of testing on society, institutions, and individuals.

(Fulcher, 2012, p. 125)

Unlike previous definitions, Fulcher's LAL conceptualization is based on qualitative and quantitative research. LAL is classified into three different categories, i. e. practical knowledge, theoretical and procedural knowledge, and socio-historical understanding, with practical knowledge serving as the foundation of LAL. This conceptualization marks a shift from a componential view (e. g. Brindley, 2001; Davies, 2008; Inbar-Lourie, 2008a) to a consideration of developmental trajectories. Admittedly, not all the components in the definition are required for all stakeholders. Similar to previous conceptualizations (e. g. O'Loughlin, 2013), this comprehensive definition does not highlight the language component in LAL, making it similar to conceptualizations of AL in general education.

D. L. Lin (2019) also proposes a comprehensive definition of LAL for language teachers. In this definition, LAL includes the following components:

- sound understanding of language and language learning;
- basic knowledge, skills, and competencies of designing, developing or evaluating classroom language assessments;
- familiarity with language assessment processes and knowing the principles and conceptions underlying assessment practices;
- engaging students in language assessments and using appropriate feedback to help learners set and achieve learning targets;
- understanding the role and function of language assessments in a specific teaching context.

(D. L. Lin, 2019, p. 13)

This definition provides some details about the unique profiles of LAL for language teachers. Yet, it is still hypothetical, representing perspectives of language assessment researchers. Nevertheless, this definition is markedly different from other conceptualizations in two aspects. First, curriculum-related assessment (Brindley, 2001) is highlighted for its greater emphasis on the language element. Second, classroom assessment, especially assessment for learning, is underscored as an important part of the assessment activities.

Becoming literate in language assessments requires a host of competencies, practical as well as theoretical, on what, why, when, and how to go about constructing a variety of assessment procedures. These competing definitions of LAL point towards divergences concerning the scope of LAL: what should be taught, and what level of expertise should be expected of stakeholders (Harding & Kremmel, 2016). Yet, clear tendencies can be detected from these definitions. First, teachers' competence in classroom assessment becomes prominent in these conceptualizations with a growing recognition of the importance of teacher-based assessment in standards-based education reform. Second, there is increasing attention to the language component in the conceptualizations.

2.2.1.2   Components of LAL

In spite of a consensus view of the significance of LAL, there has been little agreement upon what components should be incorporated in a LAL construct in the research literature, as evidenced by the different models of LAL. These models can be roughly divided into the following categories (Stabler-Havener, 2018):

- a componential model for professional development programs (Brindley, 2001);
- a knowledge-skills-principles model (Davies, 2008; Inbar-Lourie, 2008a; D. L. Lin, 2019; D. L. Lin & Gao, 2011; Pan, 2020);
- a practices-principles-contexts model (Fulcher, 2012; Jin, 2010);
- a profile model of LAL (Kremmel & Harding, 2020; Pill & Harding, 2013; Taylor, 2013).

2.2.1.2.1   A componential model for professional development programs

Brindley (2001) proposes five essential components to be included in professional assessment development programs, which focus on the knowledge base required to conduct language assessment in an educational context. These components include:

- the social context of assessment;
- defining and describing language proficiency;
- constructing and evaluating language tests;
- assessment in the language program;
- putting assessment into practice.

(Brindley, 2001, pp. 129-130)

The social context of assessment is concerned with "the social, educational, and political aspects of assessment in the wider community, including issues of ethics, accountability, and standardization as well as the role of standardized testing in society" (Brindley, 2001, p. 129). It is critical that language teachers should be aware of the social context in which the assessment is situated due to the fact that different educational contexts have different assessment values and perspectives. For instance, China is an examination-driven culture and excessive emphasis is placed on summative assessment, especially in secondary education. In addition, the social context shapes how classroom teachers and other stakeholders perceive the validity of assessment. Hence, teachers need to be aware of the social issues when designing assessments and reporting results. Ethical use of test results is also important for language teachers. With regard to the political nature of language assessments, language teachers should be aware of the way language test results are used to make decisions concerning individuals, such as classifying people, determining exclusive membership, and setting standards for success or failure to the disadvantage of certain individuals or groups (Shohamy, 1998). To minimize unintended test consequences, teachers need to avoid bias when constructing language assessments. This social perspective of assessment is in line with the "social turn" (McNamara & Roever, 2006; Shohamy, 2001) of the language assessment community, implying an epistemological shift in terms of knowledge construction and critical views on the role of language tests in society at large.

Defining and describing language proficiency is addressed as the crucial question of "what it means to know how to use a language" (Spolsky, 1985; quoted in Brindley, 2001, p. 129). As assessors of students' language performance, teachers need to examine the theoretical basis of language assessments and the various procedures involved in assessment. In doing this, teachers need to understand the concepts of reliability and validity, which serve as the basis for teachers to construct and evaluate assessments. This unit also includes a critical evaluation of models of language abilities.

The third unit—constructing and evaluating language tests—is about the development and evaluation of language tests and an introduction to statistical analysis. The fourth unit—assessment in the language curriculum—covers criterion-referenced tests and techniques associated with assessment alternatives such as portfolios, journals, self-assessments, and project work to monitor student progress and achievement, and explores how these types of assessments are integrated into the language curriculum. The final unit requires language teachers to map out a follow-up strategy for putting into practice issues raised in the previous modules with concrete test construction or assessment research projects.

These five components are modular in nature, with the first two components being core units and the remaining three optional. This is because "different individuals will require different levels of knowledge according to the nature and extent of involvement in assessment issues" (Brindley, 2001, p. 28).

2. 2. 1. 2. 2　A knowledge-skills-principles model

Davies (2008) provides a general and schematic model of LAL, which consists of skills, knowledge, and principles. Skills indicate the practical know-how of test construction and analysis; knowledge refers to the "relevant background in measurement and language description" (Davies, 2008, p. 328); principles deal with the proper use of language tests, test fairness, and impact, including questions of ethics and professionalism.

According to this model, language assessment literate teachers should know how to perform effective assessment activities, be able to ground their assessment practices on the basis of solid (descriptive) knowledge and be in a position to adopt a critical view questioning available assessment practices.

The central role of skills, knowledge, and principles in the development of LAL has been recognized and followed by other researchers. Inbar-Lourie (2008a) categorizes Brindley's (2001) assessment units in professional development programs into three key questions: the why, the what, and the how. The "why" corresponds to the first core module of Brindley's model—the social context of assessment. Language teachers need to be aware of the background and rationale of assessment. The "what" theme—the description of the trait to be assessed, applies to the second core module "defining and describing proficiency" in the program. Language teachers need to be knowledgeable in current language theories, language teaching pedagogy, and research findings regarding language knowledge and use so that they can develop assessments consistent with the current perspectives. The "how"—the method of assessment, is illustrated in the two optional units (the third and fourth), for the fifth unit extends beyond testing and assessment techniques. Different from Brindley (2001), Inbar-Lourie considers all the three optional units of assessment knowledge essential for language teachers to implement assessments skillfully in today's educational setting. She also argues for an inclusion of the language element in an LAL framework for the impact of language evaluation on civil, vocational, and educational decision making processes. The three key questions Inbar-Lourie (2008a) addresses in LAL (the how, what, and why of assessment) are in line with Davies' (2008) "skills + knowledge + principles" approach to LAL.

Based on Inbar-Lourie's (2008a) categorizations, D. L. Lin and Gao (2011) propose an expanded model of LAL. In this model, the "what" dimension covers language instructors' knowledge of subject content and prominent theories of language ability. This knowledge is reflected in teachers' understanding and awareness of reliability and validity, which is also an important part of the "what". The "why" dimension refers to the social dimension of assessment, the fairness and use of assessments. The "how" dimension mainly includes test development and analysis of assessments, design and use of classroom assessment, and assessment for learning. D. L. Lin and Gao's model (2011) expands Brindley's (2001)LAL conceptualizations by taking assessment for learning as an important part of teachers' assessment practices. Yet, D. L. Lin and Gao (2011) are not explicit in terms of the specific elements of each dimension. In addition, it is controversial whether it is appropriate to put the two key terms—reliability and validity—under the "what" dimension.

D. L. Lin (2019) also adopts Davies' (2008) "knowledge + skills + principles" approach and proposes a theoretical framework of LAL for language teachers at primary and secondary education levels.

- Knowledge: basic concepts of measurement, language system, awareness of applied linguistics
- Skills: developing, administering and scoring assessments, item analysis, reporting assessment results, providing feedback
- Principles: sensitive to local social-cultural values, assessing students to support their learning, right use of assessments, concern about fairness in assessment

In this model, the knowledge component is expanded to include not only understandings of basic terms in measurement theory, but also understandings of the language system and applied linguistics (e. g. language teaching and language learning). The principles component is ranked high to foreground the contextual nature of LAL. D. L. Lin (2019) further recommends a list of seventeen descriptors in relation to LAL requirements for Chinese primary and middle school EFL teachers. This list serves as a comprehensive checklist for EFL teachers to self-assess their competence in language assessments.

Different from previous models, D. L. Lin's (2019) model and recommended list address the LAL needs of a particular teacher population, i. e. primary and middle school EFL teachers. Different stages of education have different learning targets and expectations. They also differ in the major types of assessment activities used. This model is indicative of assessment policy initiatives in China and the contemporary assessment landscape in the globe by incorporating assessment for learning in the principles component. Moreover, the model underscores the language element, making LAL an integrated construct. As admitted by D. L. Lin (2019), however, this LAL model is speculative in nature, and its validity remains to be established in further research.

Pan (2020) decomposes the elements of LAL from a researchers' perspective. Building on depth interviews with 10 language testing and assessment experts and researchers in China, Pan suggests modifications to Davies' (2008) "skills + knowledge + principles" approach to LAL in a Chinese educational context, and proposes an additional element of "receptivity of receiving in-service LAL training". In Pan's modified model, the specific elements of the three components share more similarities than differences with previous models. In terms of receptivity of receiving in-service LAL training, it mainly refers to language teachers' willingness to accept assessment training in teacher development programs and to be involved in large-scale testing. In addition to these four basic elements, Pan (2020) suggests four factors that facilitate language teachers' LAL development in the model, i. e. linguistic knowledge, language proficiency and research literacy, educational measurement principles, and beliefs of and attitudes towards LAL.

2. 2. 1. 2. 3 A practices-principles-contexts model

Fulcher's (2012) expanded definition of LAL (in Subsection 2. 2. 1. 1) implies a hierarchy of assessment knowledge which can be conceptualized as a contextualized LAL model comprising three elements: practices, principles, and contexts (Figure 2-1). The element of practices encompasses the knowledge, skills, and abilities required for language testing practices; the principles element refers to the processes, principles, and concepts that guide language testing practices; and the contexts element includes the historical, social, and political philosophical frameworks in which the practices and principles are placed so that assessment stakeholders are able to discern the origins, reasons, and impacts for the practices and principles. In this model, the practices element serves as the foundation, and the contexts element articulates a level of complexity in LAL, which is a distinct development of previous models.

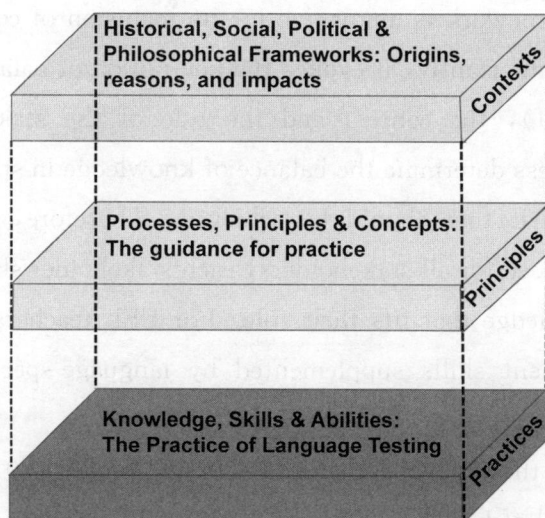

Historical, Social, Political & Philosophical Frameworks: Origins, reasons, and impacts — Contexts

Processes, Principles & Concepts: The guidance for practice — Principles

Knowledge, Skills & Abilities: The Practice of Language Testing — Practices

Figure 2-1   An Expanded Definition of LAL (Fulcher, 2012, p. 126)

The contribution of Fulcher's definition lies in a recognition that skills, knowledge, and principles are not sufficient on their own for LAL development. These three elements should be integrated in the context of assessment in a dialectical scheme between assessment constructs and historical, social, political, and philosophical frameworks. This implies that practitioners cannot be considered literate in assessment if they do not fully understand how assessment practices and contextual factors shape each other.

Taylor (2009) expands the concept of LAL to include the sociocultural dimension to account for the highly contextualized and purpose-driven nature of language assessment practice. As she points out, training for AL entails "an appropriate balance of technical know-how, practical skills, theoretical knowledge, and understanding of principles, but all firmly contextualized within a sound understanding of the role and function of assessment within education and society" (p. 27). Taylor (2009) also expands the range of stakeholders who need a level of LAL to include policy makers, government departments, and university admissions officers.

Taylor's framework is innovative for its inclusion of considerations of context. More importantly, it evokes the key notion of balance. According to Taylor (2009), the context and the role of the stakeholder in the assessment process determine the balance of knowledge in specific areas and the levels of LAL that should be achieved. Therefore, although LAL should be developed for all stakeholders, each stakeholder should acquire an amount of knowledge that fits their role. For EFL teachers, they need to develop assessment skills supplemented by language-specific assessment knowledge.

Building on the work of Fulcher (2012) and Taylor (2013), Jin (2018) proposes a model of LAL required of Chinese EFL teachers. In this model, LAL includes three components: (1) assessment knowledge, skills, and abilities; (2) assessment processes, principles, and concepts; and (3) assessment environment. Assessments are also divided into three major categories: classroom assessment, achievement assessment, and large-scale standardized testing (e. g. NMET, CET-4, CET-6). Unlike Fulcher (2012) and Taylor (2013), Jin's model (2018) allows for variation in the development of LAL components. EFL teachers need different levels of competence in different LAL components for different types of assessment activities due to the fact that different types of assessments have different purposes, methods, and content, and that teachers are involved in these activities to a varied extent (Jin, 2018). As claimed by Jin herself, this profile is proposed from a researchers' perspective and is speculative in nature. It calls for empirical research for its validity.

L. Li and Q. Wang (2020) argue that classroom assessment literacy (CAL) is the dominant literacy an EFL teacher needs to conduct language assessments. They conceptualize CAL as consisting of three components, i. e. assessment beliefs, assessment knowledge and skills, and assessment ethics. Assessment beliefs refer to EFL teachers' understanding of the purposes, processes, and functions of language assessments and the values they place on assessments. The second component refers to the knowledge of the concepts and theories of language assessment and the ability to translate them into assessment practices. When assessing students, EFL teachers need to: (1) choose and use varied assessment methods appropriate for the teaching content to elicit evidence of students' understanding of the learning goals; (2) interpret the evidence; (3) provide feedback and support to students; (4) encourage students to involve in assessment to facilitate their learning and teachers' own professional development; and (5) be ethical in assessment and avoid bias and prejudice.

2. 2. 1. 2. 4   A profile model of LAL

Pill and Harding (2013) draw on conceptualizations in scientific and mathematical literacy education and outline LAL as a continuum of five stages from illiteracy, nominal literacy, functional literacy, procedural and conceptual literacy to multidimensional literacy (Pill & Harding, 2013). Pill and Harding's model captures the fact that different stakeholders have different assessment needs, which, in turn, define the levels of assessment literacy that they should reach. The preference for describing LAL as a continuum over a dichotomy of literacy or illiteracy indicates the developmental nature of the construct and has implications for assessment training programs (i. e. LAL cannot be acquired as a block of knowledge all at once). This continuum of LAL is adopted in later studies that focus on AL levels of teachers and other stakeholders (Kremmel & Harding, 2020; Lan & Fan, 2019).

However, this continuum model of LAL is limited in the following aspects (Harding & Kremmel, 2016). First, it is not clear what levels of LAL language teachers and other stakeholders should achieve. Second, the descriptions at each level place excessive emphasis on procedural/theoretical knowledge with little reference to assessment practice. Third, the trajectory of literacy development in this continuum is not consistent with the LAL development approach proposed by Brindley (2001) and Inbar-Lourie (2008a). In Pill and Harding's (2013) scale, the philosophical, historical, and social dimensions of assessment is placed at the highest level of development, while Brindley (2001) and Inbar-Lourie (2008a) include it as a competence which should be obtained by those involved in learning about language assessment.

Yet, the characterization of multidimentionality and developmentality of LAL lays the foundation for Taylor's (2013) hypothetical profiles of LAL for different stakeholder groups (Kremmel & Harding, 2020). Taylor (2013) claims that though Fulcher's (2012) expanded working definition includes key components of the LAL construct, it does not address the breadth and depth of the components necessary for different categories of stakeholders' professional responsibilities and roles in language assessment. Taylor (2013) bridges component- and levels-based conceptualizations of LAL and proposes different levels of AL/LAL according to stakeholder constituency. As demonstrated in Figure 2-2, concentric circles expand outwards from an "expert core" of AL/LAL, with each successive ring indicating the level of competence required to meet the needs of a particular stakeholder group.

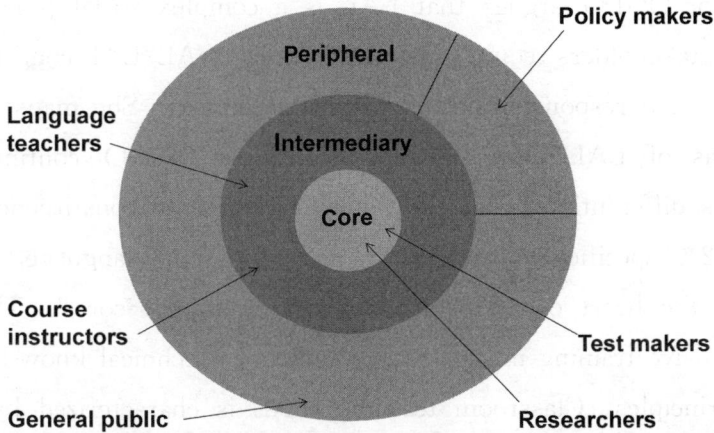

Figure 2-2   Levels of AL/LAL Differentiated According to Stakeholder Constituency

(Taylor, 2013, p. 409)

Taylor (2013) further outlines eight LAL dimensions for different stakeholder groups (test writers, classroom teachers, university administrators, and professional language testers):

- knowledge of theory;
- technical skills;
- principles and concepts;
- language pedagogy;
- sociocultural values;
- local practices;
- personal beliefs/attitudes;
- scores and decision making.

These eight dimensions are drawn from various studies and represent an attempt to "operationalize the range of key components making up the [assessment literacy/language assessment literacy] construct" (Taylor, 2013, p. 411). The inclusion of assessment beliefs and attitudes is noteworthy, echoing Breen *et al.* (1997), Leung (2014), and Scarino (2013) that teachers' beliefs about and attitudes toward assessment impact their willingness to adopt new assessment policies like formative assessment.

Taylor (2013) argues that LAL is a complex social practice, and different stakeholders require differential levels of AL/LAL congruent with their roles and responsibilities in a specific context. She maps the eight dimensions of LAL onto Pill and Harding's (2013) continuum and constructs differentiated AL/LAL profiles for four constituencies (See Figure 2-2). Specifically, test writers and professional language testers are closer to the heart of assessment—the "assessment core". They need comprehensive training in measurement theory, technical know-how, and ethical principles. Classroom teachers' LAL is characterized by greater emphasis on knowledge of assessment related to pedagogy than knowledge of language assessment theory. These profiles of LAL for different stakeholder groups offer a useful reference for a more elaborate conceptualization showing different LAL needs of different groups (e. g. Baker & Riches, 2018; Kremmel & Harding, 2020; Lan & Fan, 2019; D. L. Lin, 2019; Yan *et al.*, 2018), which, in turn, enables more focus on pedagogical efforts. Nevertheless, these different profiles are speculated from the perspective of a language assessment theorist, and the validity remains to be established. Additionally, Taylor did not provide explicit specifications of each of the dimensions. What competencies comprise the eight dimensions is left to the readers' conjecture.

To address the validity gap, Kremmel and Harding (2020) conducted an empirical study to validate Taylor's (2013) profile model by addressing LAL needs of different stakeholder groups through an international online survey. The questionnaire was developed by drawing upon assessment literature and multiple AL measures designed specifically for teachers, with its validity established through several stages of piloting and revisions. Kremmel and Harding (2020) identified nine empirically distinct dimensions of LAL:

- developing and administering language assessments;
- assessment in language pedagogy;
- assessment policy and local practices;
- personal beliefs and attitudes;
- statistical and research methods;
- assessment principles and interpretation;
- language structure, use, and development;
- washback and preparation;
- scoring and rating.

(Kremmel & Harding, 2020, p. 109)

This modified framework is generally consistent with Taylor's (2013) model, though with a few expansions (Kremmel & Harding, 2020). The two components of sociocultural values and local practices in Taylor's model are condensed into one dimension. This can be explained by the context-dependent nature of sociocultural values, which informs policy and practices in local contexts. Another noticeable distinction is the new dimension of washback and preparation, suggesting that the stakeholders are concerned about washback effect of language testing.

In Kremmel and Harding's (2020) empirical study, different stakeholder groups showed differential profiles of LAL. Language teachers perceived their assessment needs as a balanced profile with an average of level 3 (very knowledgeable) on the various dimensions. This profile basically confirms Taylor's speculation of LAL required of language teachers. However, there are three distinctions. First, Taylor considers it important for language teachers to understand local practices and sociocultural values, but it is not verified in the empirical data. Second, the utmost importance of knowledge about the relation of assessment to language pedagogy hypothesized by Taylor is not confirmed either. Third, the component of knowledge of (language) theory and understanding of assessment principles are considered more important for language teachers than in Taylor's profiles. Language testing developers' profile generally confirms Taylor's hypothesis. It is more expansive than the language teacher profile in all the dimensions except assessment in language pedagogy. Language testing researchers perceive similar assessment needs with language testing developers, but with a more balanced profile due to their complex role in assessment.

2.2.2 Studies of language teachers' LAL

A growing recognition of the significance of teachers' LAL has motivated studies that examined language teachers' assessment competencies across geographical and pedagogical contexts (e. g. Baker & Riches, 2018; Fulcher, 2012; Hamp-Lyons, 2017; Huhta *et al.*, 2005; Lam, 2015; Lan & Fan, 2019; Vogt & Tsagari, 2014; Xu & Brown, 2017; Xu & Y. C. Liu, 2009). A review of literature suggests three strands of research: language teachers' beliefs and assessment practices, measuring teachers' competence in language assessment, and professional development in language assessment (Hidri, 2021).

2.2.2.1 Language teachers' beliefs and assessment practices

The growing interest in language teachers' perceptions and practices of assessments emanates from current research strands (Shohamy *et al.*, 2008). First, there is an increasing recognition of the need to link theories of second and foreign language learning to the application of assessment as part of learning (Bachman & Cohen, 1998). Second, there is a growing understanding of the centrality of teacher-made assessments in the teaching and learning processes and of the teacher's dual role as instructor and assessor (Leung, 2004; Rea-Dickins, 2008). Third, there is growing interest in defining the nature of language ability construct (Byrnes, 2006). For instance, most EFL teachers believe in and hold positive attitudes towards formative assessment. Nonetheless, they prefer to use summative assessment techniques to measure only the product of language learning (Buyukkarci, 2014; Karagul *et al.*, 2017; Muñoz *et al.*, 2012; Serpil & Atay, 2017; Tsagari & Vogt, 2017). Also, most EFL teachers are found to test grammar and vocabulary knowledge as a sign of language development with little assessment of other language skills (Duboc, 2009; Mede & Atay, 2017; Tsagari & Vogt, 2017).

Nevertheless, compared with the profusion of research into teachers' beliefs and assessment practices in general education, relatively few empirical studies have been conducted with language teachers (e. g. Cheng *et al.*, 2008; Clarke & Gipps, 2000). Rogers *et al.* (2007) investigated with a survey the beliefs about the value of assessment and evaluation held by ESL/EFL instructors in three different contexts (Canada, Hong Kong, and Beijing). The results indicate that most teachers hold the belief that assessment and evaluation are important for instruction and help improve student learning. However, the instructors in the three contexts hold mixed, uncertain, and even contradictory beliefs of assessment, with gaps identified between assessment practices and beliefs. They tend to accept non-traditional assessment in language assessment, but actually they use traditional assessment methods more often.

Clarke and Gipps (2000) explored how teachers in primary and secondary schools in England made assessment judgments of student learning and the extent of consistency between their judgments. The results indicate that teachers adopt different assessment strategies at different grade levels and for different subjects. Specifically, mathematics and science departments in secondary schools adopt rather formal approaches to assessment, whereas English departments and primary teachers tend to use more informal, formative methods, such as student self-assessment, use of portfolios, and regular note-taking. Teachers at different grade levels also interpret the outcome statements in different ways, accounting for inconsistency in their judgment. In addition, those teachers find the assessment mechanisms (e. g. record keeping, moderation meetings) time-consuming. However, they consider moderation meetings as an essential and beneficial process that can bring about positive effects on students' learning, their teaching and assessment practices. They also express a wish to continue with teacher assessment in all its forms in spite of the extra workload.

Shohamy *et al.* (2008) investigated how teachers in secondary schools and universities perceive assessments and evaluate advanced language proficiency (ALP) learners. The results indicate that ALP teachers perceived it necessary to employ a variety of assessment methods to assess the complex ALP construct and they had a strong preference for diagnosing learners' difficulties in learning and tracking their day-to-day progress. However, there is an noticeable divergence between how teachers perceived assessment and how they practiced assessment in classroom. The ALP teachers tended to use summative assessment more often than formative and diagnostic assessments.

Muñoz *et al.* (2012) adopted surveys, written reports, and interviews to examine the assessment perceptions of language teachers in a private university. The results indicate a discrepancy between teachers' conceptions of the nature and goals of assessment and their actual assessment practices in the classroom, confirming the research findings of Shohamy *et al.* (2008). Muñoz *et al.* (2012) further suggest opportunities for teachers to reflect and self-assess their assessment practices to become aware of their own beliefs in order to bridge the gap between conceptions and practices.

Scarino (2013) examined the relationship between language teachers' tacit preconceptions, beliefs, understandings, and their development of LAL. Drawing on evidence from her previous projects, Scarino argued that teachers' personal preconceptions and beliefs about assessment formed an interpretive framework that shaped how they interpreted their own assessment practices and student learning. On the basis of this observation,

Scarino suggested that the LAL conceptualization should expand to include some components for the teachers' interpretive framework and their awareness as teacher assessor.

Z. C. Zhang and Burry-Stock (2003) is one of the few studies that examine teachers' (including language teachers) self-reported assessment practices and perceptions of their ability to perform classroom assessment in relation to different factors (e.g. content area, grade level, teaching experiences, and assessment training). The research findings indicated different factor structure for assessment practices and perceived skills in assessment, suggesting discrepancies between the two. The researchers also found that teachers' assessment practices were reflective of the nature of the subjects and grade levels they taught and that teachers with assessment training reported a higher level of self-perceived assessment skills. This has implications for assessment training. Specifically, assessment training programs should accommodate the needs of teachers working in different content areas and at different grade levels, and the assessment projects should be based on the instructional and assessment activities taking place in their own classrooms (Taylor, 1997).

Xu and L. Y. He (2019) examined how pre-service EFL teachers changed their perceptions of assessment over teaching practicum and found considerable differences in the pre-service teachers' conceptions before and after the practicum experience. These changes were related to their learning of assessment knowledge and assessment practices, echoing the research findings of Brookhart (2011) and Deneen and Boud (2014).

To sum up, these studies exploring the alignment between teachers' conceptualizations and actual assessment practices in context provide empirical support to a more contemporary understanding of LAL, which views that language assessment is a negotiated set of integrated knowledge and is enacted differently in different contexts and with different teachers (Willis *et al.*, 2013).

2. 2. 2. 2   Measuring teachers' LAL

The past decade has witnessed a growing body of research into language teachers' competence in language assessment. In these studies, self-report surveys are the most common approach (e. g. Crusan *et al.*, 2016; Fulcher, 2012; Hasselgreen *et al.*, 2004; Lan & Fan, 2019; Xu & Brown, 2017). Other studies employ mixed methods (Colby-Kelly & Turner, 2007; Gu, 2014; Jeong, 2013; Lam, 2015; Leong, 2014; Scarino, 2014; Vogt & Tsagari, 2014), whereas pure qualitative research is quite limited (Xu & Y. C. Liu, 2009).

The majority of these studies point to a low level of LAL in teachers (e. g. Boraie, 2015; Hasselgreen *et al.*, 2004; Lam, 2019; Lan & Fan, 2019). Hasselgreen *et al.* (2004) and Huhta *et al.* (2005) employed online survey to examine the actual assessment competence of three different groups of stakeholders (teachers, teacher trainers, and testing experts), and found that the three stakeholder groups lacked formal education in language assessment. Kvasova and Kavytska (2014) utilized Hasselgreen *et al.*'s (2004) survey to gauge the LAL of foreign language teachers in Ukrainian universities. The results indicated that the teachers examined were skilled in choosing ready-made language tests and providing feedback to students, but they had insufficient competence in other assessment-related activities, corroborating Hasselgreen *et al.*'s (2004) findings. Vogt and Tsagari (2014) conducted a large-scale survey to investigate the LAL levels of language teachers in Eastern Europe and found the informants had lower levels of LAL due to a lack of assessment training.

Crusan *et al.* (2016) explored EFL/ESL teachers' writing assessment competence by surveying their knowledge, beliefs, and practices of writing assessment. The results indicate a relatively higher level of assessment knowledge among these language teachers from 41 countries. Yet, they are not as confident in the use and creation of writing rubrics. Lam (2019) employed a mixed-methods approach to language teachers' writing assessment literacy and found teachers perceived a relatively low level of LAL despite the amount of assessment training received, implying that pre- and in-service teacher education programs need a clear focus on language assessment to make the program more effective.

In China, there is a growing body of research into language teachers' LAL (e. g. X. M. Li, 2020; Qiao, 2020; Shu, 2018; Y. N. Wang, 2019; Xu & Brown, 2017; Xu & Y. C. Liu, 2009; M. Zhang, 2020; Y. Zheng, 2020). Xu and Brown (2017) employed an adapted version of the Teacher Assessment Literacy Questionnair (Plake *et al.*, 1993) to investigate the AL levels of Chinese university English teachers (N=891) and found a basic level of AL in specific dimensions among these teachers. The respondents' insufficient competence in assessment is attributed to three factors: (1) a lack of assessment policies and professional standards regulating teachers' assessment practice; (2) an absence of AL requirement in teacher accreditation; and (3) inadequate pre- and in-service assessment training. Lan and Fan (2019) investigated the LAL levels of Chinese middle school EFL teachers by partly replicating the research instrument used by Vogt and Tsagari (2014). The research findings indicated that the respondents were basically functionally literate in all the five thematic areas, pointing to a gap in language teachers' LAL in technical skills and language pedagogy.

Xu and Y. C. Liu (2009) is one of the few studies that employ narrative inquiry to explore the assessment knowledge of EFL teachers in a Chinese university. Focusing on three structural conditions of teacher knowledge (temporality, sociality, and place) and their effects on teachers' construction of assessment knowledge, Xu and Y. C. Liu argue that prior assessment experience is an important factor that affects teachers' assessment practices, that power relationships in the workplace also influence teachers' assessment decision-making, and that the specific context in which assessment is conducted has an impact on teachers' sense of security and therefore the effectiveness of the assessment.

Echoing previous research, Xu and Y. C. Liu (2009) call for professional development for university EFL teachers to enhance their LAL. Other studies (e. g. X. M. Li, 2020; Qiao, 2017; Y. N. Wang, 2019; M. Zhang, 2020) examine the LAL levels of EFL teachers in primary, junior and senior middle schools, and they were generally conducted with a small number of EFL teachers from a particular geographic area. Some researchers (e. g. X. M. Li, 2020) employed an outdated questionnaire to investigate EFL teachers' LAL, while others developed an instrument without psychometric analysis, calling into question the reliability, validity, and generalizability of the research results. This calls for a valid and reliable instrument to examine EFL teachers' LAL, and at the same time, enrolling a large sample of EFL teachers from different geographic areas.

In addition to investigations of teachers' general AL/LAL levels, research is also conducted to examine whether and how teachers' demographic characteristics are related to their assessment/language assessment competence, and the research findings are mixed. Many studies point to the positive effects of assessment training on teacher AL/LAL (Alkharusi *et al.*, 2011; DeLuca *et al.*, 2013; Graham, 2005; Lukin *et al.*, 2004; Mertler, 2009). Yet, Brown (2008) and Xu and Brown (2017) suggest that assessment training experience has no (main) effect on respondent teachers' AL/LAL. In addition, no agreement has been reached on the relationship between teaching experience and AL/LAL levels, as a positive relationship is found in some studies (Hoover, 2009; Mertler & Campbell, 2004; D. H. Zheng & Ye, 2012) but not in others (King, 2010; Xu & Brown, 2017; Z. C. Zhang & Burry-Stock, 2003). Other demographics include gender (Xu & Brown, 2017; D. H. Zheng & Ye, 2012), age (Xu & Brown, 2017), teacher qualification (Hoover, 2009; King, 2010; Xu & Brown, 2017), grade levels of teaching (Z. C. Zhang &

Burry-Stock, 2003; D. H. Zheng & Ye, 2012), content areas (Z. C. Zhang & Burry-Stock, 2003; D. H. Zheng & Ye, 2012), and region (Xu & Brown, 2017; D. H. Zheng & Ye, 2012). Due to inconsistencies in research findings, there is a need to collect new evidence concerning the impact of teacher demographics on AL/LAL, especially the less researched characteristics like grade levels of teaching and geographic areas.

In these empirical studies examining language teachers' LAL, the instruments used to collect evidence about teachers' LAL are mostly based on the 1990 Standards or drawn upon existent research. Without piloting and rigorous psychometric analysis, the validity of the instruments is called into question. Meantime, cross-context LAL measures may be undesirable as assessment principles need to be relevant to the local context (Xu & Brown, 2017). New LAL measures need to be constructed to reflect current assessment standards and educational assessment research. As a response to this call, this study aims to construct an contextually-shaped LAL instrument grounded upon the assessment policy, values, and traditions within a Chinese context to investigate Chinese EFL teachers' current LAL levels and examine how the less researched demographics like grade levels of teaching and geographic areas are related to teachers' competence in language assessment.

2. 2. 2. 3   Professional development in LAL

A plethora of research has been conducted to address teachers' professional development in LAL, focusing on the assessment topics covered in education programs (e. g. Bailey & Brown, 1996; Jin, 2010), language teachers' perceived needs in assessment training (e. g. Hasselgreen et al., 2004; Fulcher, 2012; Vogt & Tsagari, 2014), and the factors that affect teachers' LAL development (Crusan et al., 2016; Yan et al., 2018). There is research on how the assessment textbook trends are catching up with practitioners' needs of assessment knowledge (J. D. Brown & Bailey,

2008).

Baker and Riches (2018) adapted Taylor's (2013) LAL model to investigate the LAL development of Haitian language teachers and external language assessment experts during collaboration. Both qualitative and quantitative data were collected to track the LAL development. The results revealed the complementary nature of expertise of language teachers and assessment specialists. Through collaboration, language teachers learned theoretical and conceptual knowledge from language testing experts and, in the meantime, provided these professionals expertise in local practice and sociocultural environment. This facilitates the LAL development of both parties.

Hasselgreen *et al*. (2004) and Huhta *et al*. (2005) employed online survey and interview to examine the actual assessment competence of three different groups of stakeholders (teachers, teacher trainers, and testing experts) and their perceived needs of training in assessment. Research findings reveal that the three stakeholder groups lack in formal education in language assessment and they express a need for assessment training in the following respects: portfolio assessment, peer- and self-assessment, continuous assessment, preparing classroom tests, interpreting test results, providing feedback, validity, reliability, statistics, item writing and item statistics, interviewing, and rating (quoted from Fulcher, 2012).

Fulcher (2012) adopted an online survey to examine the assessment training needs of foreign language teachers (n = 278). Responses to the survey demonstrated that language teachers perceived training needs in assessment components that were not incorporated in current training materials and that there was a need to include comprehensible and practical materials in order to enhance their assessment literacy. Vogt and Tsagari (2014) conducted a large-scale survey (n=853) to investigate the amount of assessment training that foreign language teachers in seven European countries received in pre- and in-service education and their perceived needs for further training. The research results indicated that these teachers had a low level of LAL and they expressed a need for assessment training. However, follow-up interviews showed that the informants were not specific about their training needs due to a lack of familiarity with assessment concepts. They also had different priorities in training in classroom-based assessment, showing the impact of educational policies and sociocultural values.

Lan and Fan (2019) adopted a modified version of the survey instrument used in Vogt and Tsagari's (2014) study to investigate the current classroom-based LAL levels, perceived needs of training in language assessments, and the gap in LAL among 344 Chinese middle school EFL teachers. The instrument, adapted into a five-point Likert scale on the basis of Harding and Pill's (2013) continuum of LAL, targeted the informants' competence in five thematic areas: (1) knowledge of theory; (2) principles and concepts; (3) scores and decision making; (4) technical skills; and (5) language pedagogy. The research findings indicated that the respondents were basically functionally literate in the five areas, pointing to a gap in language teachers' LAL in technical skills and language pedagogy when compared with Taylor's (2013) LAL profile for language teachers. The respondents expressed a need to receive further professional training to improve their understanding and practices of classroom language assessment to face increasing challenges in their teaching practices.

Research findings from these studies enable researchers and assessment training providers to identify training needs of different stakeholder groups, especially of language teachers. On a methodological note, several studies have collected teacher input using questionnaires that ask teachers to indicate the importance of various assessment topics on a Likert scale (e. g. Crusan *et al.*, 2016; Fulcher, 2012; Hasselgreen *et al.*, 2004; Vogta & Tsagari, 2014). However, as Fulcher (2012) noted, questionnaire items might elicit skewed responses in that teachers might attach equal importance to all topics out of modesty, strong motivation in LAL training, or a true lack of assessment knowledge and skills. Given the limitations of previous research, Crusan et al. (2016) called for more in-depth analysis of teachers' LAL development in relation to contextual and experiential factors.

Research also suggests that teachers' LAL is influenced by a range of contextual and experiential factors (e. g. Crusan et al., 2016; Vogta & Tsagari, 2014; Yan et al., 2018). Contextual factors include social, cultural, political, educational, and historical factors that collectively shape the assessment culture in a particular context. Experiential factors refer to those related to individuals, such as personal background, training and experience in language teaching and assessment. Crusan et al. (2016) found teaching experience was a significant factor that affected respondents' beliefs about writing assessment and AL, with more experienced teachers reporting less assessment knowledge. Ruecker et al. (2014) found that a plethora of contextual factors affected teachers' writing assessment, ranging from teachers' workloads, importance of the English writing course, availability of resources, to institutional mandates about how writing is taught and assessed. Understanding the influence of these factors can enhance our understanding of the LAL construct and its development paths for language teachers.

The research literature also highlights the fact that when teachers have a repertoire of routines to fall back on, they are more likely to use the procedures for which they have received professional development (Tsagari & Vogt, 2014). For example, Rohl's study about the influence of ESL teachers' working contexts on their use of assessment frameworks concluded that, when teachers had a choice of frameworks, they used those that they had already received training in (Rohl, 1999). This finding is corroborated by Reynolds-Keefer (2010), which revealed that trainee teachers were more likely to use scoring rubrics in their future teaching because of the experience they had with rubrics as students.

Yan *et al.* (2018) employ semi-structured retrospective interviews to investigate how contextual and experiential factors mediate in the LAL development and training needs of Chinese middle school EFL teachers. Research results suggest a highly contextualized and experiential process of LAL development, with the impact of assessment context mediated through assessment experience. Specifically, these EFL teachers develop sensitivity to teaching-testing alignment due to contextual factors of educational landscape and policies, the institutional mandates, and the assessment training resources in the local context. They construct assessment knowledge through hands-on assessment experiences and self-reflections upon those experiences. The local assessment context provides teachers with opportunities and motivation for assessment practices, and these assessment practices in turn help them to develop assessment competence, reflecting a constructivist view of LAL development (Inbar-Lourie, 2008a; Kleinsasser, 2005; O'Loughlin, 2006).

There is also a body of scholarship investigating how university-based coursework can equip pre- and in-service teachers with up-to-date assessment knowledge (DeLuca *et al.*, 2013). Regardless of the textbook trends and coursework elements, teachers find this knowledge base somewhat theoretical and pedagogically irrelevant to everyday classroom assessment practices (Popham, 2009; Yan *et al.*, 2018). Additionally, the knowledge base is mostly decontextualised, and teachers usually learn about pertinent assessment knowledge with a cookie-cutter approach. Scarino (2013) stressed the need to develop LAL for language teachers in in-service assessment education with a holistic approach that went beyond a focus on assessment knowledge. Attention needs to be directed towards the "tacit preconceptions, beliefs, understandings, and world-views about assessment that teacher-assessors bring to teacher professional learning programs and that inform their conceptualizations, interpretations, judgments, and decisions in assessment" (p. 309).

Other studies investigate how to enrich teacher assessment knowledge via coursework, professional development events, on-the-job training, and self-study via textbooks (Harding & Kremmel, 2016). Harding and Brunfaut (2020) adopted narrative inquiry to examine the trajectories of LAL development within a researcher-teacher collaboration, in which a praxis approach (integration of theory and practice) to language assessment training was employed. Both the teachers and the assessment researchers developed competence in language assessment at thematic and micro levels. Thematically, they shared a positive evaluation of the training project and, at the same time, a frustration with the environmental, political, and financial barriers that prevented a more fruitful praxis. At a micro level, the narratives revealed interesting alignments and disparities between narrators, and evidence of trajectories in agency and expertise as the project developed. Further studies are recommended to incorporate classroom-based research to better inform assessment training.

2.3 Summary

This chapter provides an extensive review of relevant studies revolving AL and LAL. From these studies, we can see different conceptualizations of AL/LAL, most of which are articulated from a researchers' perspective and thus are speculative in nature. A noticeable development in LAL conceptualizations is related to its developmental nature. LAL can be categorized on a continuum, ranging from nominal literacy to multi-dimensional competency (Pill & Harding, 2013). The depth and specific elements of expertise in a particular AL/LAL component are determined by the purpose and complexity of assessment, and discussions of LAL need to be situated in a specific educational setting, incorporating the needs of the learners assessed.

The scope of AL/LAL is dependent on the specific context. Language teachers at different grade levels (e. g. elementary, secondary, and tertiary) work in highly variant assessment contexts and may embody different LAL profiles (Yan *et al.*, 2018). Additionally, each educational setting has its own characteristics. In a Chinese educational setting, primary education is characterized by exemption from external testing. Effective EFL teachers at this level of teaching need to focus on developing pupils' interest in learning rather than measuring their learning outcomes for accountability purposes. In secondary education, however, the imposition of external, high-stakes testing (*Zhongkao* and *Gaokao*/CEE respectively) makes EFL teachers accountable to students and their parents. This requires that EFL teachers in primary and secondary education have different priorities in assessing students and they need to incorporate other body of knowledge in order to conduct assessments effectively. To arrive at a localized understanding of the set of assessment knowledge and skills prerequisite for Chinese primary and middle school EFL teachers, researchers need to place AL in the Chinese educational setting. However, little research has been conducted to address this area. The study reported in this book addresses this research gap by focusing on the assessment knowledge and skills essential for primary and middle school EFL teachers to perform language assessment tasks.

A recurring theme in earlier discussions is teachers' AL/LAL levels. Various instruments have been constructed, and many of them were built on the 1990 Standards without due attention to the current assessment landscape. Despite a growing body of research into teachers' AL/LAL levels, there are relatively few studies on Chinese EFL teachers' competence in language assessment. Among the few studies, most were conducted either with an instrument borrowed from the existent research or with an instrument developed by the researcher without establishing its validity. As LAL is contextually, socially, and culturally shaped, it is of great significance to construct a reliable and valid instrument that is appropriate for the Chinese educational setting to explore EFL teachers' current levels of literacy in language assessment. The research reported in this book intends to address this area of concern.

Among the few studies that address Chinese EFL teachers' LAL, many focus on a particular EFL teacher population, i. e. EFL teachers from primary, secondary, or tertiary education. To our best knowledge, little research examines the LAL of teachers in basic education. One of the purposes of the current study is to investigate primary and middle school EFL teachers' assessment competence and examine how it is related to such demographics as grade levels of teaching, assessment training, and institutional context. By examining the strengths and weaknesses of these EFL teachers in LAL, we are in a better position to specify their needs in assessment training. Building on these needs, pre-service education and in-service teacher professional development programs could develop language assessment training sessions to maximize the outcome of training.

CHAPTER THREE
METHODOLOGY

3.1   Research Design

This research could be understood in terms of three stages. The first stage sought to identify the essential LAL components for Chinese EFL teachers based on a comprehensive review of relevant standards documents and existing assessment literature, and sought opinions from experienced EFL teachers and domain experts for the appropriateness of the LAL model. Specifically, the answering of the first research question involved four different processes.

(1) Document and thematic analyses of different professional standards for teachers and prominent assessment standards. Standards documents that address teachers' educational assessment literacy were selected and analyzed, with an aim to analyze the themes and the changing nature of AL across countries and over time. Thematic analysis was conducted with Nvivo© (Version 11. 0) to code the documents, pinpoint and categorize the various assessment components required of teachers for effective assessment practices in the current educational accountability system.

(2) A comprehensive review of AL and LAL research to identify other bodies of knowledge and skills prerequisite for teachers in general education to conduct assessments in a professionally responsible manner and the

multitude of knowledge and skills that are specific to language teachers to conduct language assessments.

(3) Constructing an LAL model that specifies a body of assessment knowledge and skills prerequisite for EFL teachers in a Chinese educational context.

(4) Seeking domain experts' and experienced EFL teachers' judgments and comments about the completeness and appropriateness of the model.

The second stage of the research aimed to develop an LAL measuring instrument (a questionnaire). It involves five different processes:

(1) Writing items for the questionnaire;

(2) Expert judgment and teacher interviews about the items in the questionnaire, with revisions made in response to their suggestions;

(3) Piloting the questionnaire in two different stages to collect EFL teachers' responses to the items in the survey for further revision;

(4) Statistical analysis of respondents' responses to the survey (in the second piloting) to collect preliminary validity evidence of the questionnaire; and

(5) Large-scale administration of the survey to examine the psychometric properties of the questionnaire to lend further support to its validity.

The third phase analyzed EFL teachers' current LAL levels with data collected from the large-scale survey, and examined whether and to what extent demographic factors influenced their expertise in language assessment. On the basis of the findings from the survey, a follow-up questionnaire (with open-ended questions) was conducted with some participating EFL teachers to get further understandings of their conceptions of assessment, assessment practices, and assessment training experiences and needs.

3.2 Participants

The first phase of the study aimed to conceptualize the essential LAL components prerequisite for EFL teachers. To meet this end, two researchers were recruited to conduct thematic analysis of prominent assessment standards (document analysis of professional standards for teachers was conducted by one researcher). Then six experts in language assessment and six experienced EFL teachers were invited to make judgments about the completeness and appropriateness of the LAL components.

In the second research phase, an LAL questionnaire was constructed. Seven experts in language assessment and one expert in sociolinguistics were first invited to make judgments and give suggestions about the items in the questionnaire. Then a total of 624 pre- and in-service EFL teachers participated in the piloting of the survey in two different stages. After the establishment of its preliminary validity, the questionnaire was put to formal use. Altogether 835 EFL teachers answered the questions in the survey, the vast majority of whom come from different districts of Hunan and Guangdong provinces.

In the third stage of study, a follow-up questionnaire was conducted with 79 EFL teachers, who participated in the formal survey. Of these teachers, 12 are male, 69 are female; 27 teachers teach in primary schools, 24 in junior middle schools, and 30 in senior middle schools; 23 teachers work in rural schools, 29 in county town schools, and 19 in urban schools. These EFL teachers come from 3 different geographic areas in Guangdong province and 12 areas in Hunan province.

3.3 Data Collection and Analysis

Generally, a mixed-methods approach was employed to gather different types of information. Qualitative data sources included professional standards for teachers and prominent assessment standards, domain experts' and EFL teachers' judgement, interviews, and EFL teachers' responses to the open-ended questions in the follow-up survey. Document analysis was used to analyze professional standards for teachers, and thematic analysis was conducted to analyze the major components of AL in assessment standards. Interviews were conducted with EFL teachers for feedback on the knowledge or skills they needed in performing assessment-related tasks. Surveys were conducted with experts (in the first and second stages) to gather information about the extent to which they agreed upon the LAL components, the wording of the questionnaire items, and suggestions for subsequent revisions. In the second stage, experienced EFL teachers' comments were gathered via social networks (WeChat and QQ) for ambiguous and confusing wording in the LAL questionnaire before the piloting phase.

The LAL questionnaire underwent two phases of piloting before it was put into use. Based on 85 participating EFL teachers' responses to the items in the first piloting in April 2020, highly-correlated items were combined, less relevant items were removed, and some items were added in the meantime to represent the constructs in each dimension. The revised questionnaire was then piloted in late June with 539 pre-service English teachers who had one-semester practicum in primary and middle schools in the previous semester. Items with low discrimination were revised and those with negative discrimination were deleted from the questionnaire.

All the statistical analyses were performed with the software IBM SPSS (Version 26.0). An initial reliability analysis was conducted with the data from the large-scale questionnaire survey, which was followed by exploratory factor analysis (EFA) to help select items to form each of the dimensions in the LAL model. To be more specific, the data were used to examine the factor structure of the 62-item LAL questionnaire with the Principal Axis Factoring method of extraction. After factors were extracted, an attempt was made to arrive at meaningful labeling of the factors, which was then followed by a computation of the descriptive statistics for each factor. In the analysis, various criteria were used to determine the number of common factors to be retained, which included the eigenvalue-greater-than-1 criterion, the scree test, the amount of common variance explained, and conceptual interpretability of the factor structure. In addition to factor analysis, statistical analyses of participants' responses to the questionnaire were performed to gain a clear picture of EFL teachers' current levels of LAL and the influence of demographic factors on their LAL. Specifically, t-test and ANOVA were performed to examine the differences among EFL teachers in terms of grade levels of teaching, assessment training experience, and the institutional context they work at.

The follow-up survey was conducted online with wjx. cn (https://www. wjx. cn/vj/wFwiBU2. aspx). EFL teachers' responses to multiple-choice items were analyzed for frequency and percentage, and answers to open-ended questions were analyzed for themes.

3.4 Summary

This chapter provides a sketch of how the research was conducted in three different stages. Qualitative and quantitative data collected in the first two stages provide a fairly rich and deep understanding of the complex construct of LAL, and the relatively large number of participants in the piloting and formal stages lends empirical credence to the validity of the developed LAL instrument. The subsequent three chapters seek to answer the three research questions formulated in the first chapter.

CHAPTER FOUR
CONSTRUCTING AN LAL MODEL FOR
CHINESE EFL TEACHERS

The primary purpose of the current research is to construct an appropriate LAL measuring instrument for Chinese EFL teachers in primary and middle schools. As evidenced in previous chapters, LAL is a complex and multi-dimensional concept with various components subsumed under the broad construct. Hence, the first task in developing an LAL instrument is to unpack this complex construct. To meet this end, we focus exclusively on teacher knowledge and skills related to classroom-based assessment, because this is the set of knowledge and skills that teachers use on a regular basis. Standards documents (professional standards for teachers and assessment standards) were first reviewed to identify the various assessment-related components **teachers of all subject areas** need in order to assess students effectively. Then, an LAL model was proposed for EFL teachers based on analyses of the documents and relevant LAL studies reviewed in the second chapter.

4.1 Components of AL in Standards Documents

This section provides an analysis of professional standards for teachers and prominent assessment standards in response to recommendations to develop an LAL model in light of contemporary assessment standards and practices (DeLuca et al., 2016b). Standards documents in six countries

(i. e. Australia, Canada, China, New Zealand, the United Kingdom, and the United States) plus mainland Europe were selected for analysis. These English-speaking countries and regions were chosen because they are committed to the development of assessment theory, policy, and practice, and have professional standards that delineate teachers' assessment practices. China was included for its relevance to the research purpose of the current study. The analyses of professional standards for teachers and assessment standards served as a starting point for the generation of the essential LAL components, which were expected to be more aligned with teachers' current assessment needs.

Standards documents in these countries and regions were identified through a systematic review of existent assessment literature and by examining: (1) websites of governmental ministry of education, provincial department of education, public websites for national or inter-state organizations; (2) national or inter-state assessment research council, associations, and joint advisory committees; and (3) national and provincial teacher education associations. Only documents that explicitly addressed standards for teacher competence in assessment were retained for further analysis. Admittedly, the search of the standards documents was built, to a large extent, on DeLuca et al.'s review (2016b). Yet, the documents chosen for analysis in this study were the latest versions. In addition to the teacher standards documents mentioned in DeLuca et al.'s review, professional standards for teachers in Scotland and Wales were also included for their assessment policies and practices. Meanwhile, two professional standards documents for teachers in China were included for their relevance to the present study, i. e. *Professional Standards for Primary School Teachers (Trial)*[①] and *Professional Standards for Middle School Teachers (Trial)*[②].

---

① Department of Teacher Work of MoE, 2012. Professional Standards for Primary School Teachers (Trial)[S]. Beijing: Beijing Normal University Press.

② Department of Teacher Work of MoE, 2012. Professional Standards for Middle School Teachers (Trial)[S]. Beijing: Beijing Normal University Press.

4.1.1 Analysis of assessment requirements in professional standards for teachers

Ten professional standards for teachers were included for analysis. As shown in Table 4-1, three standards documents were from the United States, three from the United Kingdom, two from mainland China, and one each from New Zealand and Australian.

Table 4-1　Descriptions of Professional Standards for Teachers

Document	Description	Creator	Year
What Teachers Should Know and Be Able to Do	5 propositions	U. S. NBPTS	1989 updated in 2016
Model Core Teaching Standards and Learning Progressions for Teachers 1. 0	10 standards	U. S. InTASC	2013 updated in 2018
The New K-6 Elementary Teacher Preparation Standards	5 standards	U. S. CAEP	2018
Revised Teacher Standards	8 standards	U. K. DoE	2011 updated in 2013
Standards for Full Registration	19 standards	Scotland GTC	2012
Qualified Teacher Status Standards	18 standards and related guidelines	Wales TRA	2017
Standards for the Teaching Profession	6 standards and related guidelines	New Zealand EC	2019
Professional Standards for Teachers	7 standards and related guidelines	Australia DoE	2018
Professional Standards for Teachers (Trial)①	13 standards and related guidelines	China MoE	2012

Note: NBPTS—National Board for Professional Teaching Standards

InTASC—Interstate Teacher Assessment and Support Consortium

CAEP—Council for the Accreditation of Educator Preparation

DoE—Department of Education

GTC—the General Teaching Council　　TRA—Teaching Regulation Agency

EC—Education Council　　MoE—China's Ministry of Education

---

① Professional Standards for Teachers (China) refer to the standards documents for primary and middle school teachers collectively.

The coverage of AL in these standards documents differs considerably in terms of specificity. Some documents make specific reference to the use of assessments in the teaching process, while others refer to assessment generally with no further guidance about how to assess students and how to make use of assessment results to inform teaching. Table 4-2 presents a quick snapshot to illustrate how specifically this set of teacher standards documents address the topics identified within the three broad types of assessments: formative assessment, classroom-based summative assessment, and external summative assessment. This presentation is based on Kahl *et al.*'s (2013) assessment literacy framework whereby literacy in assessment is evaluated in terms of three dimensions: types of measures, quality of measures, results and their use. In this table, the codes G, S, and N are used to indicate the extent to which these standards incorporate AL components. Specifically, a G indicates general inclusion of the respective AL components in the standards, an S indicates more specific representation of the corresponding components of AL, and an N indicates no evidence of AL components in the standards.

In coding reference to AL components, the following guiding question is used to determine the assignment of a G, S, or N to each teacher standards document: "When thinking about the AL component 'types of measures'/'quality of measures'/'result and use', is the standards document too general or specific enough to inform the development and use of quality assessment tasks for teacher candidates or practicing teachers?" A close look at Table 4-2 shows the visibility of formative assessment and classroom-based summative assessment in the dimension of "types of measures", generally or specifically, in all the ten teacher standards documents examined. Note that there are no standards documents that we think warrant classification as specific reference to external summative assessment, and only two of the standards documents reference generally to this type of assessment.

Table 4-2   References to AL Components in Professional Standards for Teachers

AL Components	Source of document	FA	CBSA	ESA
Types of Measures Standards differentiate between types of assessment measures.	U. S. -NBPTS (2016)	G	G	G
	U. S. -InTASC (2018)	S	G	N
	U. S. -CAEP (2018)	S	G	N
	U. K. -DoE (2013)	G	G	G
	Scotland-GTC (2012)	G	G	N
	Wales-TRA (2017)	G	G	N
	New Zealand-EC (2019)	G	G	N
	Australia-DoE (2018)	S	S	N
	China-MoE (2012)			
	-Primary school	G	N	N
	-Middle school	G	N	N
Quality of Measures Standards reference how to develop quality measures and/or judge the quality of measures.	U. S. -NBPTS (2016)	G	N	N
	U. S. -InTASC (2018)	S	G	N
	U. S. -CAEP (2018)	S	G	N
	U. K. -DoE (2013)	N	N	N
	Scotland-GTC (2012)	N	N	N
	Wales-TRA (2017)	G	G	N
	New Zealand-EC (2019)	N	N	N
	Australia-DoE (2018)	S	S	N
	China-MoE (2012)			
	-Primary school	N	N	N
	-Middle school	N	N	N
Result and Use Standards reference how to appropriately use assessment results.	U. S. -NBPTS (2016)	S	G	N
	U. S. -InTASC (2018)	S	G	N
	U. S. -CAEP (2018)	S	G	N
	U. K. -DoE (2013)	G	G	G
	Scotland-GTC (2012)	G	G	N
	Wales-TRA (2017)	G	G	N
	New Zealand-EC (2019)	G	G	N
	Australia-DoE (2018)	S	S	N
	China-MoE (2012)			
	-Primary school	G	N	N
	-Middle school	G	G	N

Note: FA—formative assessment   CBSA—classroom-based summative assessment
      ESA—external summative assessment

"Quality of measures" is the single dimension where none of the standards documents make reference to external summative assessment, since most practicing teachers are not involved in developing external testing. This is also the AL component where the greatest discrepancies reside. First, teacher standards documents of New Zealand, the United Kingdom, Scotland, and China do not refer to formative or summative assessment. Second, Australian teacher standards document makes specific reference to qualities of both formative and classroom-based summative assessments. Third, the CAEP standards and the InTASC Model Core Teaching Standards make specific reference to qualities of formative assessment, but general reference to qualities of classroom-based summative assessment. Fourth, NBPTS standards makes general reference to qualities of formative assessment only.

In terms of the component "result and use", the document of the United Kingdom is the only one that makes general reference to the result and use of all three types of assessments. The three standards documents of the U. S. make specific reference to the result and use of formative assessment, general reference to classroom-based summative assessment, and no reference to external summative assessment. The standards of Scotland, Wales, and New Zealand are similar in the sense that they make general references to the result and use of formative and classroom-based summative assessments and no reference to external testing. The Australian standards document refers specifically to both formative and classroom-based summative assessment, but makes no reference to external summative assessment. It merits our attention that China's *Professional Standards for Primary Teachers (Trial)* is the single document that makes reference only to the result and use of formative assessment.

Table 4-3 is a visual display of the percentage of teacher standards documents that make reference to AL components in the three types of assessments. In terms of formative assessment, all the documents refer to the types of measures and result and use of formative assessment. To be specific, three standards documents (30%) make specific reference (S) to types of measures and seven documents (70%) make general reference (G) to it. Three documents (30%) make specific reference (S) to quality of measures, and 30% of the documents make general reference (G) to it. Four documents (40%) make specific reference (S) to result and use, and six (60%) make general reference (G) to it.

Table 4-3   Percentage of References to AL Components in Teacher Standards

AL Component	FA		CBSA		ESA	
	S	G	S	G	S	G
Types of Measures	30%	70%	10%	90%	0	20%
Quality of Measures	30%	30%	10%	30%	0	0
Result and Use	40%	60%	10%	80%	0	10%

Note: FA—formative assessment   CBSA—classroom-based summative assessment
ESA—external summative assessment

When it comes to classroom-based summative assessment, one and the same standards document (Australia-DoE, 2018) (10%) refers specifically to the three AL components; nine of the ten standards documents (90%) make general reference to types of measures, three (30%) to quality of measures, and eight (80%) to result and use. It is interesting to note that none of these teacher standards documents make specific reference to the three AL components of external summative assessment. Nevertheless, two of the ten standards documents (20%) make broad reference to types of measures, and one (10%) refers generally to result and use.

To sum up, current trends in education reform point to an increased use of data, along with growing demands for educators at all levels to be assessment literate. Based on the descriptions and analyses above, we can see that assessment components are visible in all the ten teacher standards documents examined. Teachers need to demonstrate a basic understanding of assessments and recognize the importance of formative assessments.

They need to know varied types of assessment methods, the merits and limitations of each method. It is also essential for teachers (in different career stages and at different levels of education) to employ assessment methods appropriate to their purposes to monitor students' progress and use assessment information to facilitate teaching and learning.

These documents feature elements related to effective and appropriate use of student assessment. They incorporate and place more emphasis on formative assessment to reflect the changing education landscape worldwide. Meanwhile, most of these standards documents address formative and classroom-based summative assessments and don't cover external summative assessment.

Given our analysis above, we can come to several conclusions about the ten teacher standards documents regarding assessment components.

(1) There is a tendency to underscore formative assessment, yet with general references to the construct.

(2) Formative and classroom-based summative assessments are often used together, with no differentiation between the two.

(3) Standards are lacking for knowledge about external summative assessment.

(4) Most standards lack the breadth and depth of assessment knowledge and skills for a teacher to be effective in assessment practices.

Considering the significance of AL in the teaching profession and the lack of details necessary to provide guidance for teachers, we need to review prominent assessment standards to have a rich and complete understanding of the full spectrum of assessment knowledge and skills prerequisite for teachers.

4.1.2 Thematic analysis of assessment standards

This subsection provides an analysis of prominent assessment standards documents that address standards of assessment practices. Eight governmental and research-informed assessment standards documents are included and displayed in Table 4-4 in order of publication year.

Table 4-4   Assessment Standards Documents

Document	Description	Creator	Year
The Standards for Teacher Competence in Educational Assessment of Students	7 standards	U. S. AFT, NCME, & NEA	1990
Principles for Fair Student Assessment Practices for Education	5 principles and related guidelines	Canada JAC	1993
Code of Professional Responsibilities in Educational Measurement	8 standards and related guidelines	U. S. NCME	1995
Changing Assessment Practices: Process, Principles and Standards	15 standards and related guidelines	U. K. ARG	2008
Brookhart's updated lists	11 standards	Brookhart	2011
European Framework of Standards for Educational Assessment 1. 0	7 core elements	Europe AEA-Europe	2012
Standards for Educational and Psychological Testing	19 standards	U. S. AERA, APA, & NCME	2014
Classroom Assessment Standards: Practices for PreK-12 Teachers	16 standards and related guidelines	U. S. JCSEE	2015

Of these assessment standards documents, five are from the United States and one each from Canada, the United Kingdom, and mainland Europe. Some of these documents are intended primarily for classroom teachers, such as the 1990 Standards, Brookhart's updated list, and *Classroom Assessment Standards: Practices for PreK-12 Teachers*. Others are developed primarily for professional test developers, but they are applicable to classroom teachers' assessment practices or have implications for classroom teachers.

A standard thematic coding procedure was employed to analyze inductively the eight assessment standards documents with the software NVivo© (Version 11. 0). All the documents were first coded by primarily intended users, types of assessments addressed, and publication year. The unit of thematic analysis was each standard and its guidelines, if there was any, in the document. Different from DeLuca *et al.*'s analysis (2016b), the supporting research-based explanations of each standard statement and its associated guidelines were also referenced in the coding process to have a richer and deeper understanding. The standard and its guidelines were coded under different nodes if they contained different categories of information.

4. 1. 2. 1　Codes and themes in the assessment standards documents

All the assessment standards documents were coded digitally by the author and one Ph. D. student specializing in language assessment, and the Kappa (agreement) coefficient was . 78. The disagreements in coding were then discussed to reach consensus. Finally, 43 child nodes (codes) were identified across the eight documents. These codes were categorized into eight parent nodes (themes) as follows:

- assessment purposes: choosing assessment forms according to instructional decisions;
- assessment processes: the various stages involved in assessment practices;
- assessment for learning (AfL): using assessments to facilitate teaching and learning;
- content knowledge: knowledge of a subject/discipline;
- pedagogical content knowledge (PCK): knowledge of what to teach in a particular subject and how to teach it;
- test fairness and ethics: fair treatment of all students and protecting the rights of those concerned;
- measurement theory: psychometric properties of tests;

• assessment education and support for teachers in assessments: support for teachers' AL development.

Table 4-5   Codes and Themes of Assessment Standards Documents

Themes	Codes	Theme Descriptions
Assessment purposes	Assessment of learning vs. Assessment for learning Classroom-based vs. Standardized testing Multiple forms of assessment	Choosing assessment forms according to instructional decisions
Assessment processes	Choosing assessment methods Designing/developing assessments Administering assessments Collecting information Scoring assessments Developing valid grading procedures Analyzing students' performance Monitoring and revising assessment Interpreting assessment results Communicating assessment purposes/processes Communicating assessment results Using assessment results to make decisions	The various stages involved in assessment practices
Assessment for learning	Formative assessment Diagnostic assessment Student self- and peer-assessment Providing effective feedback to students Student engagement in assessment practices Student use of assessment information Using assessments for instructional planning	Using assessments to facilitate teaching and learning
Content knowledge	Students having opportunity to learn the material Learning intentions/outcomes Learning progressions	Knowledge of a subject/ discipline
Pedagogical content knowledge	Knowing general principles of how students learn a particular content area	Knowledge of how learning happens

Table 4-5 (continued)

Themes	Codes	Theme Descriptions
Test fairness and ethics	Disclosing accurate, balanced information Protecting rights and privacy Minimizing biases Complying with standards Employing fair assessment practice Fair representation of students' achievement Accommodating exceptional learners Acknowledging diversity	Fair treatment of all students and protecting the rights of those concerned
Measurement theory	Reliability Validity Norms and standards	Psychometric properties of tests
Assessment education and support for teachers in education	Professional learning activities/training Professional development in AL Collaboration Reflection on assessment practices	Support for teachers' AL development

4. 1. 2. 2   Comparison between different types of assessment standards

Table 4-6 displays the distribution of the coded themes in each of the assessment standards documents examined. These documents were arranged first in terms of primarily intended users (professionals vs. classroom teachers), then in order of publication year. Specifically, the NCME (1995), AEA-Europe (2012), and AERA, APA, and NCME (1990) documents are set up for the professionals who develop standardized testing. The JAC (1993) document is intended for both classroom teachers and professionals, but the thematic analysis of this document is restricted to the part concerned with classroom assessment by teachers. The four documents developed by AFT, NCME, and NEA (1990), ARG (2008), Brookhart (2011), and JCSEE (2015) respectively are intended for classroom teachers and address classroom assessment, summative or formative, or both.

Table 4-6   Distribution of themes in assessment standards document

Theme	1995 NCME	2012 AEA-Europe	2014 AERA, APA, & NCME	1990 AFT, NCME, & NEA	1993 JAC	2008 ARG	2011 Brookhart	2015 JCSEE
Assessment purposes	1(20)	1(14.3)	1(5.3)	2 (28.6)	1(20)	3(20)	3(18.2)	2(12.5)
Assessment processes	7(80)	7(85.7)	6(63.2)	8 (85.7)	9(100)	5(46.7)	6(27.3)	7(31.3)
AfL	—	—	—	—	—	4(33.3)	3(27.3)	6(31.3)
Test fairness and ethics	7(80)	—	2(10.5)	1(14.3)	2(60)	—	1(9.1)	5(18.8)
Content knowledge	—	—	—	—	—	—	2(27.3)	1(6.3)
PCK	—	—	—	—	—	—	1(27.3)	—
Measurement theory	2(40)	—	4(21.1)	2(14.3)	—	—	3 (9.1)	2(6.3)
Education & support for teachers	—	—	2(15.8)	—	—	3(13.3)	1(9.1)	1(6.3)

Note: The first numeral represents the number of different codes in a theme for a particular document; the numeral in parenthesis indicates the percentage of standards covered by the theme in question. — indicates no coverage of a theme in the document.

For each document, the number of different codes under a theme was computed to show the extent of representation of that theme. The proportion of standards (in relation to the total number of standards in a particular document) representing this theme was displayed as a percentage in parenthesis to indicate the density of the theme. This proportion-based representation of theme density minimized the inflation effect of frequency counts across documents which have varied numbers of standards and/or guidelines (DeLuca & Bellara, 2013). Table 4-6 shows all these documents address assessment purposes and processes in spite of varying density of representation. These documents are also markedly different from each other in terms of coverage of other themes. The subsequent analysis is based on types of documents in terms of primarily intended users.

Documents intended for professionals: The NCME(1995) document aims to help professionals in clarifying assessment purposes (20%), becoming familiar with the various assessment processes (80%), conducting assessments in a fair and ethical manner (80%), and understanding measurement terms (40%). The AEA-Europe (2012) document focuses exclusively on assessment purposes (14.3%) and assessment processes (85.7%). By contrast, the AERA, APA, and NCME (2014) document is dedicated to more themes of assessment: assessment purposes (5.3%), assessment processes (63.2%), test fairness and ethics (10.5%), measurement theory (21.1%), and education and support for teachers (15.8%). The AERA, APA, and NCME (2014) is also the only document that incorporates assessment education and support for teachers in assessment. This finding points to the reality that, though there are expectations for teachers to become competent in assessments, few documents are in place to support teacher learning in assessment (DeLuca et al., 2016b).

Documents intended for classroom teachers: The AFT, NCME, and NEA (1990) document has similar focuses with the NCME (1995) document, nevertheless with different density of representation for assessment purposes (28.6%), assessment processes (85.7%), test fairness and ethics (14.3%), and measurement theory (14.3%). The JAC (1993) document focuses on three themes: assessment purposes (20%), assessment processes (100%), and assessment fairness and ethics (60%). The three documents of ARG (2008), Brookhart (2011), and JCSEE

(2015) address both classroom-based summative assessment and formative assessment, but they have different focuses. To be specific, the ARG (2008) document addresses assessment purposes (20%), assessment processes (46.7%), assessment for learning (33.3%), and education and support for teachers (13.3%). Brookhart's (2011) updated list is the most encompassing document in that it represents all the eight themes: assessment purposes (18.2%), assessment processes (27.3%), AfL (27.3%), test fairness and ethics (9.1%), content knowledge (27.3%), PCK (27.3%), measurement theory (9.1%), and assessment education and support for teachers in assessment (9.1%). The JCSEE (2015) document is also comprehensive for its representation of seven of the eight themes: assessment purposes (12.5%), assessment processes (31.3%), AfL (31.3%), test fairness and ethics (18.8%), content knowledge (6.3%), measurement theory (6.3%), and assessment education and support for teachers in assessments (6.3%).

It merits our attention that the two documents, i. e. AFT, NCME, and NEA (1990) and JAC (1993), though intended primarily for teachers, share more features with those set up for professionals. This is due in large part to the fact that these two documents address primarily standardized testing and summative assessments. All the five assessment standards documents concerning formal testing dedicate, to a substantial degree, to assessment processes with a proportion-based density ranging from 63.2% to 100%. In summary, the eight assessment standards documents represent different themes due to different primary target users and types of assessments covered.

4. 1. 2. 3　Shifts in assessment standards for teachers over time

This subsection takes a close look at the shifts in assessment standards intended primarily for classroom teachers. There are five documents which can be classified into this category, i. e. AFT, NCME, and NEA (1990),

JAC (1993), ARG (2008), Brookhart (2011), and JCSEE (2015). These documents are divided, in terms of publication year, into two groups for further analysis: 1990—2005, and 2006—present.

1990—2005: Both documents in this category were developed in the 1990s, and the themes identified are assessment purposes, assessment processes, test fairness and ethics, and measurement theory. The primary theme is assessment processes, including choosing assessment methods, developing assessment methods, administering assessments, collecting information, developing valid grading procedures, communicating assessment purposes and processes, scoring assessments, interpreting assessment results, using assessment results to make decisions, and communicating assessment results to students, parents, etc. These documents focus on helping teachers choose, develop, and use assessments, mainly summative and standardized testing, in order to make sound and fair educational decisions about students. In this period, assessment standards documents centered on standardized and classroom-based summative assessment with an emphasis on developing teachers' understandings of summative forms of measurement. This focus is understandable for its correspondence with the implementation of standards-based education reform and accountability testing in the U. S.. The two documents further incorporated the themes of test fairness and ethics (14. 3% in AFT, NCME, and NEA, 1990, 60% in JAC, 1993). The JAC (1993) document places much emphasis on test fairness and ethics because the principles and associated guidelines presented in this standards document are intended to strive for fair and equitable assessment of all students. The AFT, NCME, and NEA (1990) document also identifies the theme of measurement theory (14. 3%).

2006—present: Assessment purposes, assessment processes, test fairness and ethics, and measurement theory are still identified, and assessment processes remain to be the central theme in these three documents. Nevertheless, these themes are represented to a lesser extent and new themes are identified. First, AfL emerges and has become a dominant theme in these assessment standards documents (33.3% in ARG, 2008; 27.3% in Brookhart, 2011; and 31.3% in JCSEE, 2015). In particular, the JCSEE (2015) document has 6 different codes under this theme. The AfL theme extends the conceptions of assessment beyond summative and standardized testing (DeLuca *et al.*, 2016b). It underscores the importance of teachers' competence in assessment practices, which include formative and diagnostic assessments, providing effective, immediate feedback to students, engaging students in assessment practices and in use of assessment results, self- and peer-assessment on the part of students, and instructional planning based on student performance.

A second change in the documents in this period is the emergence of the theme of assessment education and support for teachers in assessment (13.3% in ARG, 2008; 9.1% in Brookhart, 2001; 6.3% in JCSEE, 2015), indicative of a growing awareness that teachers' AL needs to be developed with opportunities for formal learning in assessment. Provision of opportunities for teachers to promote their AL has been recognized as a critical component in developing effective teachers. This finding makes sense given the paradigm shift in assessment and the increasing emphasis on AL in current assessment landscape. A third notable change is related to the emergence of the two themes of content knowledge (27.3% in Brookhart, 2011; 6.3% in JCSEE, 2015) and PCK (27.3% in Brookhart, 2011). This is not surprising given the growing emphasis on the integration of assessment with content area and pedagogy to guide formative assessment.

Overall, the thematic analysis of the eight assessment standards documents demonstrate significant changes in the characterization of assessment competencies for teachers (DeLuca *et al.*, 2016b). From Table 4-6, we can see that the prominent assessment standards documents centering upon formal testing have different focuses from those addressing classroom-based summative and formative assessments. Generally, the former documents place more emphasis on assessment processes, illustrating the importance of conducting assessment practices in a professionally responsible manner, while the latter documents are more concerned with how to use assessments to document and facilitate student learning. On the other hand, the shifts of assessment standards for teachers over time reveal the increasing importance of AfL and a growing awareness of providing assessment education and support for teachers to develop assessment competent teachers.

4.2   LAL Knowledge and Skills Prerequisite for EFL Teachers

With theoretical insights gained from literature review and standards documents analysis, the LAL construct was defined and a theoretical model was proposed. This section first gives an account of experienced EFL teachers' comments about the completeness of the definition and domain experts' feedback on the completeness, clarity, and relevance of the LAL definition and model that could inform subsequent revisions. Then it turns to the conceptual and operational definitions of the dimensions of the model to lay a solid foundation for the creation of questionnaire items in the following chapter.

4.2.1   Conceptualizing LAL components for EFL teachers

The preliminary LAL definition was first sent to six experienced EFL teachers. They were asked to list the factors that they took into consideration when assessing students. Generally, these teachers had different considerations when designing assessment tasks, depending on the grade levels of teaching. However, most teachers would give thought to learners' age-related characteristics, cognitive factors, learning status as well as their attitude toward and interest in learning English. They would draw upon their knowledge of students when making decisions and providing feedback, encourage students and give them a sense of progression.

For the validation of the LAL definition and framework, opinions were solicited from domain experts at home and abroad. Foreign experts were identified by reviewing articles in such prominent journals as *Language Testing*, *Language Assessment Quarterly*, *The Teacher Educator*, and *Teaching and Teacher Education*. These experts have publications which address AL or LAL and are cited by many other researchers in the assessment community. Domestic experts were identified by their monographs and publications in prominent international journals (the aforementioned) and Chinese journals like *Foreign Language Teaching and Research*, *Journal of Foreign Languages*, *the Foreign Language World*, *Modern Language Journal*, etc. Altogether, 12 experts in language testing and assessment were identified.

A questionnaire-like method was employed to gather domain experts' quantitative and qualitative feedback. The questionnaire was emailed to these experts in early April 2020, asking the expert participants to rate the extent to which they agreed with the definition and component structure of the theoretical framework on a five-point Likert scale (strongly disagree— strongly agree). In addition, the experts gave suggestions for revision and explained their reasons for proposing them. For better communication, a Chinese version of the questionnaire was sent to Chinese experts. Six experts replied (four Chinese and two foreigners) and provided constructive feedback. All these experts have a doctorate in language assessment or educational assessment. For the sake of convenience, the four Chinese experts were identified as C, L1, L2, and X respectively and the foreign experts were identified as B and H.

Overall, the six experts differed considerably in terms of their agreement with the definition. Experts L1, X, and H have a research orientation in AL/LAL. They expressed overall agreement (with a rating of

4) with the definition. In the meantime, experts L1 and X offered some suggestions for revision, emphasizing the goal of English teaching at different levels of education and the characteristics of language teaching and learning in a Chinese educational context.

Expert L1: EFL teachers also need to encourage students to involve in assessment. They need to make students gain a sense of progression in assessment and hence develop an interest in learning English.

Expert X: In terms of feedback to students and their parents, the teachers need to provide it not just timely, but also **appropriately.**

Experts L2 and C have varied research interests. Generally, expert L2 expressed general agreement with the LAL definition and model, while expert C had different judgment. For this reason, he was the only expert that provided detailed and constructive feedback in two rounds. In the first round, expert C rated "undecided" in terms of the acceptability of the definition, mainly concerned about the way LAL was conceptualized and its comprehensiveness and systematicity.

> This definition includes many assessment-related elements, but it is not standard in form. The content is not systematic or complete, either. You can incorporate the three basic questions in formative assessment (i. e. Where are we going? Where are we now? And how do we get there? *added by the researcher*) in the definition to make it more systematic. In terms of the form it takes, it is better to conceptualize the construct in this way: LAL is defined as a set of theoretical, methodological knowledge and skills that EFL teachers need in order to assess effectively students' language use abilities and capacity for language learning in relation to the learning objectives, and to provide useful feedback to them. Specifically, ...
>
> To make the definition complete, you can consider adding the following elements: (1) language ability; (2) language learning capacity; (3) feedback to students about their current learning status;

(4) feedback about how to respond to the assessment evidence; (5) knowledge of theories of language, language learning, language development, teaching, and measurement; (6) methodology, both quantitative and qualitative; and (7) more technical skills of assessment.

Foreign expert B did not quite agree with the definition. Some of his suggestions were not relevant to the Chinese educational context. Yet, several pieces of his advice were pertinent.

In an AfL context, teachers need to be skilled in interacting with and interpreting exchanges with students and devising activities by which students assess themselves and peers. .... maintaining pupils' joy and motivation in language learning should not be the primary goal of feedback. Feedback must focus on providing valid and reliable information about how to improve and how to evaluate one's learning. ... encouraging pupils to involve in assessment and giving them a sense of progression in language learning are supposed to be two different skills and thus need to be separated.

With these experts' constructive feedback, the LAL definition underwent major revisions and was resent to expert C for further feedback in mid-April 2020. The revised definition was not sent to the other experts because expert L1, L2, X, and H basically agreed upon the preliminary definition, and expert B was not familiar with English education in the Chinese context. In the second round, expert C basically agreed with the revised definition, and provided some minor suggestions.

The teacher also needs to be able to assess students' learning outcomes. ... Current research into feedback emphasizes the importance of remedies. You'd better incorporate this in your definition. ... In "a set of knowledge, skills, and abilities", "skill" is a subordinate to "ability". You had better remove "ability" from the definition. ... "letting students participate in assessment" is not appropriate, since "letting sb do sth. " is not a skill anyhow.

With these further suggestions from expert C, the LAL construct was conceptualized as a set of knowledge, skills, and principles EFL teachers need in order to assess effectively students' language learning in relation to the learning objectives, language use abilities, and capacity for language learning, and to provide immediate, appropriate, and useful feedback to them. Specifically, an assessment literate Chinese EFL teacher:

(1) is familiar with language learning objectives against which to assess students;

(2) is familiar with the various components of language knowledge and ability and understands how these components are developed;

(3) is aware of students' cognitive and affective characteristics in language teaching and assessment;

(4) understands student' language learning processes and their capacity for language learning;

(5) is familiar with assessment processes and different assessment methods;

(6) is aware of the principles and ethic considerations that guide language assessments;

(7) is skilled in choosing, designing, and scoring classroom language assessments and communicating assessment results appropriately to pupils and their parents;

(8) gets students to involve in assessments;

(9) assesses effectively students' language learning outcomes and gives them a sense of progression;

(10) provides timely and useful feedback to students; and

(11) makes evidence-informed adjustments in instruction and facilitates

students' learning.

4.2.2　Development process of the LAL model

Built on the comprehensive definition and research literature, an LAL model was developed. This model included six dimensions: knowledge of assessment in language pedagogy, knowledge of linguistics and applied linguistics, awareness of students' cognitive and affective characteristics, personal beliefs of and attitudes toward assessment, technical skills in assessment, and assessment principles & ethic considerations.

Generally, five of the experts agreed on the model. Expert C, however, was critical of this preliminary model, arguing it was merely a list of components without illustrating how they were connected to each other. Therefore, Davies' (2008) "skills + knowledge + principles" approach was adopted and the model was modified with specifications of the connections among the dimensions. Expert C further gave some comments on the adjusted model. First, it was not appropriate to put under knowledge the dimension personal beliefs of and attitudes towards assessment. This dimension did not belong to any of these categories. Second, for better judgments about this model, it was advisable to utilize the default shapes (i. e. circles or ovals for latent variables, rectangles for observable variables) to represent the various components and dimensions and be more clear about what the different shapes and arrows in the diagram mean. Expert C further recommended Weir and Khalifa's (2008) reading framework for reference in terms of the interconnections of the various components in the model.

With expert C's continuous, constructive feedback, the dimension of personal beliefs of and attitudes towards assessment was removed from the preliminary model. In the revised model (Figure 4-1), LAL is conceptualized as a multi-dimensional, dynamic construct which involves the knowledge, skills, and principles components.

Knowledge：

- knowledge of assessment in language pedagogy
- knowledge of linguistics and applied linguistics
- awareness of students' cognitive and affective characteristics

Skills：

- technical skills in assessment

Principles：

- assessment principles & ethic considerations

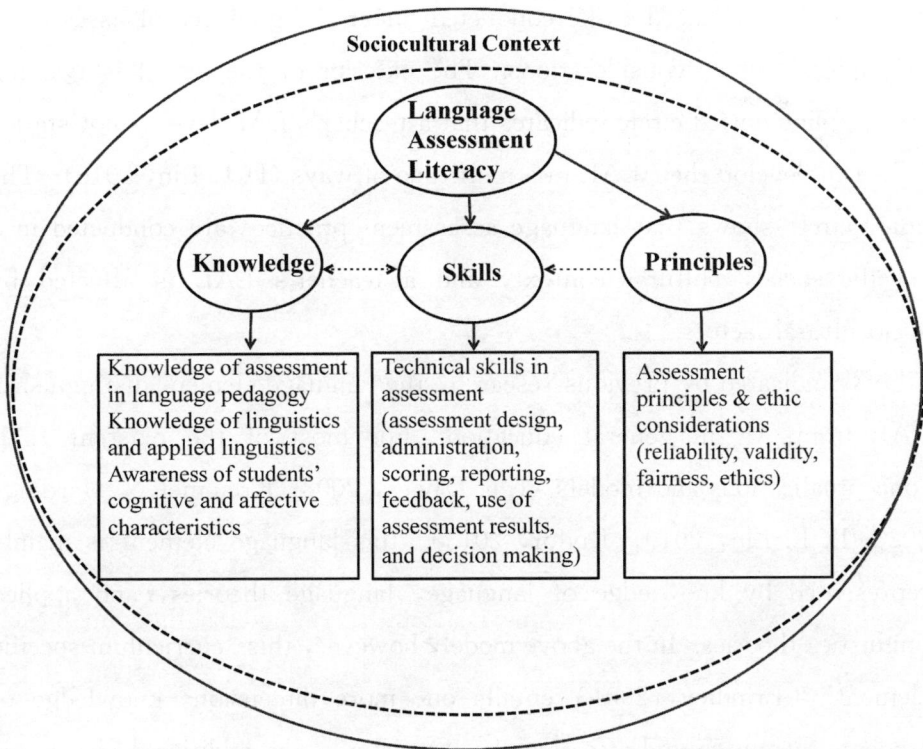

Figure 4-1   **LAL Model for Chinese Primary and Middle School EFL Teachers**

In the model above, knowledge, skills, and principles are linked as a system in this structure, cobbled together in response to task demands. Knowledge serves as the basis of skills, and the enhancement of skills facilitates the increase of knowledge (indicated by the dotted double-headed arrow). Specifically, an assessment literate EFL teacher needs, first of all, to possess some knowledge of assessment in language pedagogy. In the same vein, an EFL teacher also has to have some basic understandings of language and how the English language is taught and learned. In the process of language teaching and assessment, an EFL teacher further builds knowledge about language and language assessment. Principles affect skills at more of a macro level (represented by the dotted single-headed arrow). A teacher's assessment skills are manifested in the various assessment processes, which need to be conducted under the guidance of assessment principles & ethic considerations. The exterior of the model is two big circles. The dotted circle indicates that a teacher's LAL level is not static. S/he can develop their LAL in a multitude of ways (D. L. Lin, 2016). The outer circle shows that language assessment practices are conducted in a specific social, cultural context, and a teacher's LAL is affected by sociocultural factors.

As indicated by previous research, the language element distinguishes LAL from AL in general education. For most of the existent LAL conceptualizations and models (e. g. Davies, 2008; Kremmel & Harding, 2020; D. L. Lin, 2019; Taylor, 2013), this language element is mainly represented by knowledge of language, language theories, and applied linguistics theories. In the above model, however, this "curriculum-specific element" (Brindley, 2001) entails one more dimension—knowledge of students' cognitive and affective characteristics. The additional element is related to the reality that English is taught and learned in China as a foreign language, where students have little contact with people who speak the language. This accounts for the fact that most Chinese students find it rather difficult to learn the foreign language and get frustrated easily in language learning. This fact entails that the set of assessment knowledge and skills required of an effective Chinese EFL teacher is somewhat different from that of an effective teacher in an educational context where English is learned as a second language. Underpinning effectiveness in assessment practices is EFL teachers' capacity to integrate knowledge of language assessment and students' cognitive and affective characteristics. To be specific, Chinese EFL teachers need to be aware of students' cognitive and affective characteristics and give them a sense of progression in language assessment. The teachers also need to motivate students to learn the language with assessments and after assessments.

4.2.3   Nature and range of the contents of the constructs in the model

Another purpose of the current study is to develop a measuring instrument based on the LAL conceptualization to assess the LAL levels of Chinese primary and middle school EFL teachers. The creation of an item pool is a complex process. It requires a clarification of the nature and range of the content of the construct (Clark & Watson, 1995) for a systematic sampling of content that is potentially relevant to the target broad construct. This subsection elucidates both conceptual and operational definitions of the constructs in the broad concept of LAL, which can be seen in Table 4-7, 4-8, and 4-9 respectively.

Table 4-7   Specifications of the Knowledge Component

Dimension	Construct	Conceptual Definition	Operational Definition	Rationale
Knowledge of assessment in language pedagogy	Knowledge of assessment in language pedagogy	Understanding how assessment is related to language teaching and learning.	Understanding why and how EFL teachers conduct assessment in the language classroom.	National English Curriculum Standards (MoE, 2012, 2017); Professional standards for teachers

Table 4-7 (continued)

Dimension	Construct	Conceptual Definition	Operational Definition	Rationale
Knowledge of linguistics and applied linguistics	Knowledge of linguistics	Understanding the basic components of language and language abilities.	Understanding the basic structure of language, the components of language knowledge and language abilities; understanding the level of language abilities that students at a particular level of education are expected to achieve.	National English Curriculum Standards (MoE, 2012, 2017); Kremmel & Harding (2020); D. L. Lin (2019)
	Knowledge of applied linguistics	Basic understanding of foreign language teaching and learning strategies, and the cognitive processes involved in foreign language learning.	Knowledge of foreign language teaching includes three aspects: teaching approaches, strategies and methods that are effective for students; knowledge of how to develop students' language knowledge and abilities; and knowledge of the curriculum objectives. Knowledge of cognitive processes in foreign language learning mainly refers to an understanding of how emotional and motivational factors affect students' foreign language learning and the role of our mother tongue in foreign language learning.	Kremmel & Harding (2020); D. L. Lin (2019); Scarino (2013) Ellis(1994); Gardner & Lambert (1972); Csizér & Dörnyei (2005); Dörnyei (1998, 2003); Gardner (2001); Cai (2019)

Table 4-7 (continued)

Dimension	Construct	Conceptual Definition	Operational Definition	Rationale
Awareness of students' cognitive and affective characteristics	Cognition	In the process of foreign language learning, cognitive aspects include the thinking processes and mental procedures involved. Cognitive factors that influence learning range from basic learning processes, such as memorizing facts or information, to higher-level processes, such as understanding, application, analysis, and evaluation.	Cognitive factors are operationalized as such functions as attention, memory, and reasoning.	McKay (2006); Danili & Reid (2006)
	Affect	Affect is considered as aspects of emotion, feeling, mood, or attitude which condition behaviors in second language acquisition (Pavlenko, 2005, p. 34).	Affective factors include attitudes, motivation, anxiety, and self-esteem.	Ellis(1994); Pastore & Andrade (2019) C. M. Wang (1991)

As shown in Table 4-7, the knowledge component covers three dimensions: knowledge of assessment in language pedagogy, knowledge of linguistics and applied linguistics, and awareness of students' cognitive and affective characteristics. Assessment in language pedagogy refers to how assessment is related to and integrated in language teaching. From a curriculum standards perspective, this can be understood in terms of how and why EFL teachers conduct assessments in actual classrooms. In Kremmel and Harding's (2020) research, this dimension is used to represent partly the different purposes that teachers assess students and the various methods to meet these ends. Partly is used here mainly because Kremmel and Harding's (2020) survey was intended for different stakeholder groups (language teachers, researchers, language testing professionals, etc.) and the language learning context is different from that in China.

The second dimension in the knowledge component includes two constructs: knowledge of linguistics and knowledge of applied linguistics. Knowledge of linguistics refers to an understanding of the basic components of language and language abilities. From a curriculum standards perspective, EFL teachers need to have a basic understanding of the components of language knowledge (e. g. knowledge of phonetics, grammar, vocabulary, functions, topics, discourse, and pragmatics) and language abilities (e. g. listening, speaking, reading, writing, and viewing). In Kremmel and Harding's study (2020), knowledge of the basic structure of language is also an important part of language knowledge. D. L. Lin (2019) goes further to suggest that an effective language teacher should be (moderately) knowledgeable of the CSE, which provides a clear framework and guidance for classroom assessment. Hence, the construct of knowledge of linguistics is operationalized as an understanding of the basic structure of language, the components of language knowledge and language abilities, and the level of language abilities that students at a particular level of education are expected to achieve (as described in the CSE).

The construct of knowledge of applied linguistics is broad in scope. Since most frontline EFL teachers might lack systematic knowledge of theories, this construct is narrowed to contain two sub-constructs: basic understanding of foreign language teaching and learning strategies and knowledge of the cognitive processes involved in foreign language learning. In China, *National English Curriculum Standards* (MoE, 2017, 2022) serve as the guideline of English language teaching in basic education. The documents outline unequivocally the objectives of English teaching at different stages of learning. In many teacher education programs, *National English Curriculum Standards* has been offered as an obligatory course for pre-service English teachers. According to the curriculum standards, EFL teachers need to use skillfully and creatively teaching methods and design effective instructional activities to help students develop basic knowledge in the English language and competence in language skills. In the meantime, EFL teachers need to incorporate individual differences of learners when designing teaching and assessment activities. Knowledge of how language knowledge and skills are developed is also a source of items in LAL surveys (e. g. Kremmel & Harding, 2020), and components of reference framework of LAL (e. g. D. L. Lin, 2019).

In terms of the cognitive processes involved in foreign language learning, motivation and interest are important components of students' emotion and attitude. Emotion and attitude constitute one of the five components of comprehensive language use abilities in *English Curriculum Standards for Compulsory Education* (MoE, 2012), and serve as fundamental components of students' language learning capacity as stipulated in *English Curriculum Standards for General High School* (MoE, 2017). Hence, EFL teachers need to be aware of the critical roles that motivation and interest play in effective foreign language teaching and learning. In the meantime, the influence of one's native language on foreign language learning process is also significant (Cummins, 1979; Ellis, 1994; Schumann, 1997; Skehan, 1998), especially when learners begin to learn the language.

Operationally in this study, knowledge of foreign language teaching includes three aspects: effective teaching approaches, strategies, and methods that are appropriate for students at a particular phase of education, knowledge of how to develop students' language knowledge and abilities, and knowledge of the English curriculum objectives. Knowledge of cognitive processes in foreign language learning mainly refers to an understanding of how emotional and motivational factors affect students' foreign language learning and the role of the native language in foreign language learning.

The third dimension of the knowledge component is awareness of students' cognitive and affective characteristics. A multitude of factors affect students' language learning, and cognition and affect are of crucial importance in this process. Cognitive factors refer to the characteristics of the person that may improve or hinder his performance and learning (Danili & Reid, 2006). In the process of foreign language learning, cognitive aspects include the thinking processes and mental procedures involved. Cognitive factors that influence learning range from basic learning processes such as memorizing facts or information to higher-level processes like understanding, application, analysis, and evaluation. In this book, cognitive factors are operationalized as such functions as attention, memory, and reasoning.

Of equal importance with cognition in language learning is affect (Stern, 1983). Affect is considered as aspects of emotion, feeling, mood, attitude, and self-esteem which condition behaviors in second language acquisition (Pavlenko, 2005, p. 34). The impact of affect can be positive or negative, depending on the emotion, attitude, etc. the student has. In this study, affective factors refer to attitudes, motivation, anxiety, and self-esteem. Different from learning a second language, foreign language learning takes place in a context where the target language is seldom used outside the classroom. Foreign language learning is much less effective and students may get frustrated and discouraged. To facilitate student learning, EFL teachers need to spend a considerable amount of time to help students consolidate what they have learned, and at the same time, pay close attention to the affective responses of learners.

The skills component, as indicated in Table 4-8, incorporates one dimension—technical skills in assessment. According to prominent assessment standards documents outlined in Chapter 4, technical skills in assessment refer to those skills involved in the process of assessment, ranging from developing assessment methods and tasks to making use of assessment results. This dimension places more emphasis on formative assessment than on summative assessment for its inclusion of making use of assessment results to facilitate learning and providing feedback.

Table 4-8   Specifications of the Skills Component

Dimension	Construct	Conceptual Definition	Operational Definition	Rationale
Technical skills in assessment	Technical skills in assessment	The various skills involved in assessment processes.	An assessment literate teacher should be skilled at: choosing and developing appropriate assessment methods and tasks; communicating assessment procedures and purposes to students; developing appropriate scoring schemes and grading students' performance; describing and reporting assessment results to students and their parents; providing immediate and appropriate feedback to students; making use of assessment results to inform teaching and learning; and getting students involved in assessment.	Assessment standards documents; research literature (e. g. Kremmel & Harding, 2020; D. L. Lin, 2016; Fulcher, 2012; Vogt, 2014; Mertler, 2013)

Specifically, an assessment literate teacher should be skilled at:
- choosing and developing appropriate assessment methods and tasks;

- communicating assessment procedures and purposes to students;
- developing appropriate scoring schemes;
- grading students' performance;
- describing and reporting assessment results to students and their parents;
- providing immediate and appropriate feedback to students;
- making use of assessment results to inform teaching and learning;
- getting students to involve in assessment.

These skills are important components of LAL questionnaires (e. g. Kremmel & Harding, 2020; D. L. Lin, 2016; Fulcher, 2012; Vogt & Tsagari, 2014) and AL surveys, especially those developed on the basis of the 1990 Standards (e. g. O'Sullivan & Johnson, 1993; Mertler, 2003; Mertler & Cambell, 2005; Plake et al., 1993; Zhang & Burry-Stock, 1997).

The third component of the model is assessment principles & ethic considerations (Table 4-9). This refers to EFL teachers' understanding of or actions towards appropriate use of language assessment and consequences in language assessment, including reliability, validity, fairness and ethics (Butler et al., 2021; Davies, 2008; J. Y. Lee, 2019; J. Y. Lee & Butler, 2020). Reliability indicates the degree of consistency of assessment results. Validity is a very complex concept and its definition is evolving (J. D. Liu & M. Z. He, 2020). For classroom assessment, which is criterion-referenced, validity refers to the alignment of assessment tasks with curriculum and teaching objectives. Assessment studies abound that lack of assessment training is a prevalent fact in global teacher education. Even for those teachers who have received some training in educational assessment or language assessment, it is still difficult for them to understand key measurement terms, especially reliability and validity. Hence, the construct of assessment principles is operationalized as how EFL teachers demonstrate their understanding of reliability and validity in actual assessment practices when it comes to investigating whether they observe these assessment principles.

Table 4-9　Specifications of the Principles Component

Dimension	Construct	Conceptual Definition	Operational Definition	Rationale
Assessment principles and ethic considerations	Assessment principles	Assessment should be reliable and valid. Reliability indicates the degree of consistency of assessment results. For classroom assessment (criterion-referenced), validity refers to the alignment of assessment tasks with curriculum and teaching objectives.	How EFL teachers demonstrate their understanding of reliability and validity in actual assessment practices.	Assessment standards documents; research literature (e. g. Kremmel & Harding, 2020; D. L. Lin, 2016; Fulcher, 2012; Vogt, 2014; Mertler, 2003)
	Ethic considerations	Language assessment should be fair and ethical to students. By fairness, it means equity of treatment and absence of bias. In terms of ethics, it refers to legal and ethical responsibilities concerning the use of assessments.	How EFL teachers observe fairness and ethics principles in actual assessment practices.	Assessment standards documents; research literature (e. g. Brookhart, 2011; Xu & Brown, 2016)

The ethic considerations element is an important facet in many assessment standards. It is an umbrella term in this study that covers fairness and ethics. According to Bachman and Palmer (2010), fairness includes equity of treatment and absence of bias. That is, students should receive fair treatment in assessment and the assessment tasks should not be biased towards a particular group of students. By ethics, it means that EFL teachers need to understand legal and ethical responsibilities concerning the use of assessments. For instance, EFL teachers should protect students' privacy to assessment results as well as their rankings. They also need to accommodate the needs of those special students. For the sake of clarity, the construct of ethic considerations is operationalized as how EFL teachers observe fairness and ethics principles in actual assessment practices.

4.3　Summary

This chapter first provides a comprehensive analysis of the assessment components in standards documents. Built on these standards documents and existent research studies, the LAL construct was defined in a way appropriate for the Chinese educational context, and a preliminary model was proposed to illustrate the various assessment knowledge and skills EFL teachers need to be effective in classroom assessment of students' language learning. This model underwent inquiries from experts in the assessment community, and the input and support from these scholars lent credence to its validity. The constructs in the model were elucidated to lay a solid foundation for the development of an LAL measuring instrument in the subsequent chapter.

CHAPTER FIVE
DEVELOPMENT AND VALIDATION OF AN LAL MEASURING INSTRUMENT

The development of a measuring instrument is a complex and iterative process. This chapter reports this process in two sections. The first section gives an account of experts' review of the survey items and the whole questionnaire, and describes how the questionnaire was piloted at the various stages of development. The second section is mainly concerned with the sources of the items in the pool and the layout of the questionnaire. With the pooling of items in the questionnaire, an attempt was made to establish construct validity of the survey in the third section. A large-scale online survey was launched to collect empirical evidence from EFL teachers at primary and middle schools in different districts of two provinces in mid- and south China. Exploratory factory analysis (EFA) was then performed to analyze the factor structure of the items. The psychometric properties of the scale and the sub-scales were also examined.

5.1   Development Process of the Questionnaire

In Chapter 4, the constructs in the proposed LAL model were defined both conceptually and operationally. These specifications served as the starting point for the creation of the item pool. For a systematic sampling of content that might comprise the constructs, relevant literature was reviewed and sources from which potential items might be drawn/developed for the pool were identified. These sources included various kinds of standards documents (e. g. curriculum standards, professional standards for teachers, assessment standards), AL/LAL surveys, and other research studies. Based on these sources, a multi-item scale was created for each dimension. This initial item pool underwent several stages of development, and the refining process spanned about four months, beginning in early March and ending in mid-July in 2020. Figure 5-1 is a rough sketch of this process.

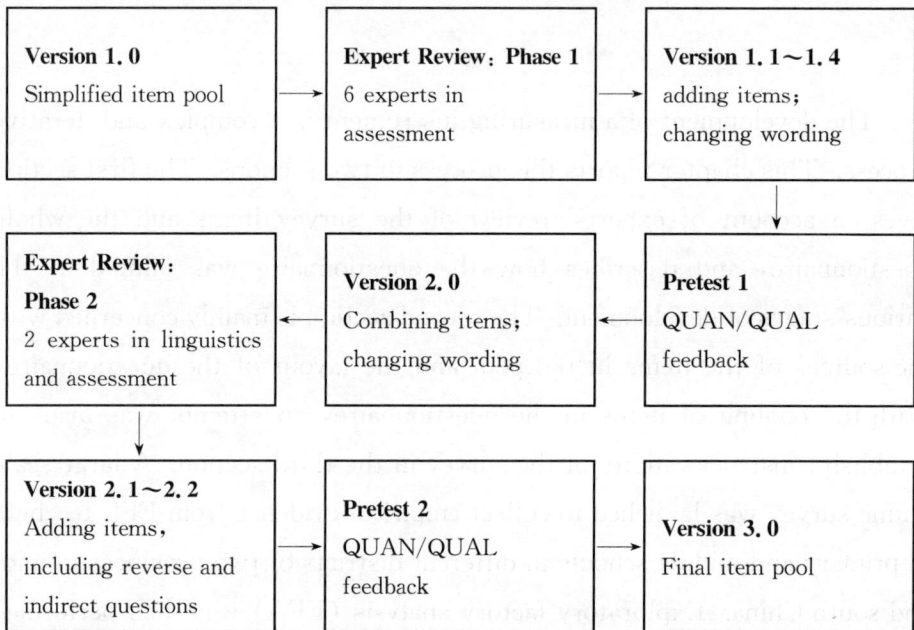

Version 1. 0 Simplified item pool	**Expert Review: Phase 1** 6 experts in assessment	**Version 1. 1~1. 4** adding items; changing wording
Expert Review: **Phase 2** 2 experts in linguistics and assessment	**Version 2. 0** Combining items; changing wording	**Pretest 1** QUAN/QUAL feedback
Version 2. 1~2. 2 Adding items, including reverse and indirect questions	**Pretest 2** QUAN/QUAL feedback	**Version 3. 0** Final item pool

Figure 5-1   Stages of Developing the LAL Questionnaire

The initial item pool consisted of 41 items and served as the basis of expert review. The experts recruited for the first review were the ones that provided constructive feedback about the LAL definition and theoretical model in Chapter 4. Emails were sent to these experts, who were requested to judge the extent to which they agreed with the items in each subscale and the whole questionnaire on a five-point Likert scale (strongly disagree to strongly agree) and to suggest any revisions to the questionnaire. For better communication, a Chinese version of the item pool was emailed to the Chinese experts. This process yielded numerous suggestions for revising the item wording and the overall scale for completeness, representativeness, and cohesion.

In terms of individual experts' feedback, expert B deemed the survey problematic. However, many of the revisions that he suggested were more relevant to external large-scale testing (e. g. knowing how to calculate, interpret, and evaluate validity evidence for assessment processes; knowing how to evaluate the validity of interpretations made from assessment result by conferring with colleagues or comparing to other data), and thus were not reported here. He was also most concerned about the wording of items and suggested using appropriate verbs to indicate and distinguish items targeting different dimensions.

Experts L1, L2, and X, however, basically endorsed this survey with a rating of 4 to the whole item pool. They also suggested several revisions. Specifically, expert L1 and L2 thought it was necessary to add items to measure Chinese EFL teachers' understanding of the CSE. In the current educational assessment reform, classroom teachers were expected to be able to evaluate students' English language ability. The CSE served as a frame of reference in terms of what language learning objectives could be identified and what achievement standards could be set. EFL teachers needed to be familiar with the different levels and descriptors. Expert L1 also pointed out that the ability to conduct holistic assessment was more relevant to primary EFL teachers. This subpopulation of EFL teachers did not assess pupils' listening, speaking, reading, and writing skills separately due to students' limited language proficiency. The items that tapped into EFL teachers' ability to assess the four language skills might not be appropriate.

Expert X provided many suggestions. These suggestions could be classified into five categories as follows:

- Avoiding items that were too general (e. g. how to involve students in peer- and self-assessment);

- Items targeting the same dimension needed to be parallel in form;
- Avoiding overlapping between items;
- The wording of items needed to be in line with the construct; and
- Items should be placed under the most relevant dimension.

Expert C was undecided upon the item pool. He provided the most feedback before the survey was first piloted. Actually, he reviewed the item pool three times in the first phase and gave detailed feedback each time. The following is a summary of his suggestions for revision:

- More items to be developed;
- Reducing overlapping of items;
- Keeping balance in the number of items for each dimension;
- Changing wording of some items;
- Avoiding double-barreled questions; and
- Indirect questions for abstract constructs.

In terms of the first suggestion for revision, expert C suggested more items to be developed to well represent the constructs in the two dimensions: technical skills and knowledge of linguistics and applied linguistics. He also suggested strategies to analyze whether the constructs were well represented. For the second suggestion, there should be a balance of items for the constructs in the same dimension as well as for each dimension. Specifically, more items needed to be developed to highlight the language element. The wording of some items also seemed to be problematic to expert C. On one hand, the wording of items addressing the construct of assessment principles was too technical. They needed to be revised to be accessible to EFL teachers, and examples could be provided when necessary. On the other hand, there should be specific verbs in front of each item to indicate the developer's intention. For instance, items that addressed assessment-related knowledge and assessment principles & ethic considerations should begin with such words or expressions as knowing, understanding, familiar with, aware of, etc. to distinguish them from those measuring assessment-related skills. Expert C also suggested indirect questions for abstract constructs (i. e. those items should examine how EFL teachers translated their assessment knowledge and skills into practice rather than measure their knowledge and skills directly).

With all the constructive feedback, major revisions were made to the item pool and Versions 1. 1~1. 4 were produced. Version 1. 4 was then piloted via social media Apps (WeChat and QQ) and wjx. cn for qualitative and quantitative feedback. In terms of qualitative feedback, 7 EFL teachers were recruited to provide detailed feedback about clarity and accessibility of the items. These teachers came from different schools in three provinces (Hunan, Guangdong, and Gansu), and most of them were the author's former students. After careful reading of the questionnaire, they found 22 items problematic (difficult to understand or answer). These teachers voiced their understandings and provided suggestions for revision.

With all these revisions, the questionnaire (59 items) was then piloted with 78 in-service EFL teachers from Hunan and Guangdong provinces. Some bonuses were offered via WeChat red envelops to increase respondents' interest in the survey. Statistical analysis of the 65 valid surveys showed that there was a significant order effect with the questionnaire. Respondents gave quite similar responses to the items under the same dimension (which were grouped together). Consequently, the reliability coefficient (alpha) of the scale was close to 1, and extremely high correlations were detected between some items addressing the same construct. Similar items were then merged, and Version 2. 0 of the questionnaire (45 items) was produced.

In the second phase of expert review of the questionnaire, expert Y was recruited. Expert Y had a Ph. D. degree in sociolinguistics. Emails were sent to expert Y, who chose to provide his feedback through WeChat voice chat. There were two recorded voice chats with expert Y, one in mid-May, and the other in early June. Each chat lasted about 40 minutes, and expert Y gave detailed comments on the questionnaire locally and globally. In his first review, expert Y's feedback boiled down to three aspects: insufficient items, lack of reverse questions, and uniformity of items.

Expert Y suggested more items be included to well represent the dimensions. In order to better judge the representativeness of the constructs, he advised the author to list the theoretical or empirical source of each construct and its conceptual and operational definitions and to develop a minimum of two or three items for every construct. He also emphasized the need to include a few reverse questions, indirect items, and even contextualized items to triangulate the constructs. In terms of the dimension awareness of students' cognitive and affective characteristics, expert Y deemed it necessary to include items that highlighted the features of English teaching and learning in a Chinese context. He was also critical of the uniformity of item types, suggesting adding multiple-choice items. However, this advice was not taken for the need to establish the internal structure of the questionnaire.

With expert Y's constructive feedback, the constructs in each dimension were defined both conceptually and operationally with a specification of their theoretical or empirical sources (see Section 5. 2. 2). On the basis of these specifications, 17 more items were designed (including reverse and indirect questions) and the wording of some items was revised. This process yielded Version 2. 1, which was then sent back to expert Y for a second review in early June. Generally, expert Y was positive about the revised questionnaire, and provided the following suggestions for improvement.

- The scope of the operational definition of each construct was narrower than that of the conceptual definition. This narrowing of scope needed to be justified.
- Some items were ambiguous and needed to be piloted with EFL teachers.
- The unbalanced 5-point Likert scale for the items targeting the knowledge component needed to be changed into a balanced one.
- The reverse questions needed to be justified, i. e. what was the theoretical basis of each item?

• Contextualized items were preferred for difficult constructs.

These suggestions were adopted for Version 2. 2 (60 items), which was piloted with 9 pre-service EFL teachers for qualitative feedback. These pre-service teachers were senior English education majors from three normal universities in Hunan province, and they had conducted one-semester teaching practicum (*Dinggang internship*) at primary schools, junior and senior middle schools in the previous semester. In these individual and group meetings (off-line meeting with pre-service teachers at the university where the author worked and online meeting with others), the pre-service teachers were asked to read carefully before answering the items and to make comments if the items were unclear to them or if they had any difficulty in understanding the terminology in the items. Altogether eight items were found to be problematic. These items were either unclear or had terminology which was difficult to understand. Based on this feedback, further revisions were made and another piloting was conducted of the changed version online with a larger population of pre-service EFL teachers.

The data collection spanned a period of 22 days. A total of 530 respondents participated in the survey. Removing those responses which were identical for all the items, or finished in less than 200 seconds, or had a mean value greater than 4. 5, there left 172 valid responses. The rate of valid responses was low mainly because of respondents' low interest in the questionnaire on one hand, and a lack of reward for participation on the other hand. Some participants also commented that there were too many items to respond to in the survey and it took them too much time.

Statistical analysis of the valid responses showed the survey was highly reliable with a Cronbach α coefficient of .956. EFA was conducted by employing different criteria and the most parsimonious and conceptually interpretable factor structure was obtained when extracting 6 factors wherein 5 factors were retained (Table 5-1). The factor structure was basically in line with the five dimensions of the revised LAL model proposed in Chapter 4. Given that the questionnaire needed further revision, the labeling of each factor was left to the validation stage.

Table 5-1　Direct-Oblimin Rotated Five-factor Solution of Initial Questionnaire

Item	Factor 1	Factor 2	Factor 3	Factor 4	Factor 5
Item 22	.717				
Item 23	.716				
Item 20	.693				
Item 31	.656				
Item 32	.653				
Item 26	.597				
Item 28	.577				
Item 30	.568				
Item 25	.550				
Item 29	.542				
Item 24	.513				
Item 13		−.739			
Item 12		−.639			
Item 7		−.632			
Item 8		−.625			
Item 14		−.623			
Item 5		−.575			
Item 2		−.565			
Item 9		−.541			
Item 11		−.535			
Item 3		−.453			
Item 60			.685		
Item 58			.584		
Item 59			.539		
Item 16				.618	
Item 10				.615	
Item 15				.496	
Item 17				.418	
Item 46					.692
Item 41					.636
Item 49					.521

In terms of the items in the survey, there were low to moderate correlations between items, and the item-total correlation statistics demonstrated that most of the items were discriminative, with the highest index being .749 for Item 60. However, six items were detected to be of low discrimination. Item 48 and 56 had an index ranging from .2 to .3, Item 34, 37, and 40 had a value between .1 and .2, and Item 49 had a discrimination indicator close to .05. The wording of Item 34, 40, 48, and 56 was then changed. Item 49 remained unchanged because this was a reverse question and was borrowed from an existent survey (D. L. Lin, 2016). Item 37 was removed, however, for its low relevance to the construct. In the meantime, 3 more items were added.

An analysis of the mean showed that respondents tended to rate high on the scale. Opinions were then sought from Dr. Z, an expert in language testing and assessment. Her feedback focused on the wording of items addressing assessment-related knowledge, which began with "I know/I think..." . Dr. Z claimed that such wording increased the probability of social desirability in responding to questionnaire items, i. e. respondents tend to endorse the items by choosing the positive end of the scale. With this constructive feedback, those items were changed into questions beginning with "what is.../ how to..." and the final version (Version 3. 0) was produced.

5.2   Final Item Pool of the Questionnaire

There were 62 items in the final version of the questionnaire. Specifically, ten items were designed to examine the constructs in Dimension 1, nine items to examine the constructs in Dimension 2, twenty items targeting those in Dimension 3, twelve items targeting the constructs in Dimension 4, and eleven items for those in Dimension 5. This section provides a detailed description of the sources, types of the survey items, and layout of the questionnaire.

5.2.1 Sources of the items

Table 5-2 shows the sources from which 53 of the items were created (the other nine items were discussed later). In this subpool, a few items (mainly those targeting the constructs in Dimension 1) were borrowed from existent surveys (e. g. Kremmel & Harding, 2020; D. L. Lin, 2016). Borrowing is considered as a good way of designing quality items because the borrowed items have been piloted and validated (Dörnyei & Taguchi, 2010; Qin, 2009). Some other items were adapted to make them appropriate in a Chinese educational context. For instance, for items measuring EFL teachers' knowledge of how to get students to involve in assessment, a specific example was provided to illustrate the steps in peer- or self-assessment. Nevertheless, more than half the items were developed, which were theoretically rooted in research studies, assessment standards, and professional standards for teachers.

Table 5-2   Sources of Questionnaire Items

Dimension	Sources	Item No.
Knowledge of assessment in language pedagogy	Krememel & Harding (2020)	1, 3, 7, 8, 10, 11, 13
	Professional standards for teachers	2, 13
	National English Curriculum Standards (MoE, 2012, 2017)	1, 2, 3, 7, 8, 10, 11, 13
	Vogt & Tsagari (2014)	1, 13
Knowledge of linguistics and applied linguistics	Krememel & Harding (2020)	15
	English Curriculum Standards for Compulsory Education (MoE, 2012)	9, 17
	English Curriculum Standards for General High School (MoE, 2017)	6,12
	D. L. Lin (2019);	9,17,18
	McKay (2006)	19
	Yang & Wu (2018)	18

Table 5-2 (continued)

Dimension	Sources	Item No.
Technical skills in assessment	Prominent assessment standards	20, 21, 23, 24, 25, 26, 27, 28, 29,56
	Professional standards for teachers	22, 28, 31
	English Curriculum Standards for Compulsory Education (MoE, 2012)	
	English Curriculum Standards for General High School (MoE, 2017)	31, 33
	Vogt & Tsagari (2014)	30, 33
	Bachman & Palmer (2010)	28
	Kremmel & Harding (2020)	26
	Fu (2010)	49
	Peng et al. (2014)	33
Awareness of students' cognitive and affective characteristics	Professional standards for teachers (U. S., U. K., Australia, China)	54, 61
	English Curriculum Standards for Compulsory Education (MoE, 2012)	41, 48
	English Curriculum Standards for General High School (MoE, 2017)	34, 36, 38, 39, 41, 48
	Krememel & Harding (2020)	35, 46
	Peng et al. (2014)	35, 36, 44
	Fu (2010)	41, 43
	McKay (2006)	40
	Vogt & Tsagari (2014)	36
Assessment principles & ethic considerations	Prominent assessment standards	45, 58, 59, 62
	English Curriculum Standards for Compulsory Education (MoE, 2012)	51, 52, 55, 57, 60
	English Curriculum Standards for General High School (MoE, 2017)	51, 52, 55, 57, 60
	Bachman & Palmer (2010)	60, 62
	Kunnan (2004)	62
	D. L. Lin (2016)	45, 47
	Giraldo (2018)	55

In Table 5-2 above, prominent assessment standards and professional standards for teachers are umbrella terms used to refer to those standards documents analyzed in Chapter 4. As can be seen, the items in the survey have a variety of sources. First, they are based on prominent assessment standards, professional standards for teachers, China's *National English Curriculum Standards* (MoE, 2012, 2017), and many research studies, though the major sources are standards documents and *National English Curriculum Standards* (MoE, 2012, 2017), which provide a theoretical basis for more than half the items. Second, many of these items have more than one source. The assessment standards serve as sources for items addressing technical skills in assessment and assessment principles. Nevertheless, these assessment standards are not the only sources of these items. As outlined in the second chapter, many conceptualizations of AL/ LAL underscore the importance of these technical skills and assessment principles. For the sake of space, these studies are not listed as sources in the table. Some other examples are Item 1, 3, 7, 8, 10, 11, and 13. Though they are borrowed from Kremmel and Harding (2020), we could also trace these items to China's *National English Curriculum Standards* (MoE, 2012, 2017).

There are 62 items in the questionnaire, and Table 5-2 only displays the sources of 53 items. The other nine items are not directly traceable to existing studies or standards documents. Thus they are not listed in the table above. Four of the nine items (Item 4, 5, 16, 14), which are subsumed in the dimensions of assessment in language pedagogy and knowledge of linguistics and applied linguistics, are intended to highlight the Chinese educational context in which the survey is intended to be used. They focus on EFL teachers' knowledge of assessment requirements at the micro, meso, and macro levels, the overall objectives of the English curriculum, and the CSE descriptions of primary and middle school students' general language abilities. These four items are included because, as argued by researchers (e. g. Xu & Brown, 2016), assessment practices are conducted in a specific sociocultural context, and a teacher's LAL is defined and affected by the social cultural factors.

5.2.2   Negatively worded and indirect questions

Another five items that are not listed in Table 5-2 are Item 37, 50 for Dimension 3 and Item 32, 42, 53 for Dimension 5. Item 37 (I am not concerned about the deviation of students' scores when I describe language test results.) is related to Item 21 (I am able to describe language test results.). In the normal running of things, a complete description of scores on a summative test should include indicators of central tendency and dispersion of scores. Deviation, or standard deviation in a more strict sense, is the most essential index of dispersion of scores. Item 37 is negatively worded, focusing on the negative rather than positive aspect of the target construct. Negatively worded items are usually included in a questionnaire to make a balanced mixture of items. A balanced survey can effectively avoid a response set in which the respondents choose only one end of a rating scale, and reduce the harmful effects of the acquiescence bias in the meantime(Dörnyei & Taguchi, 2010; Qin, 2009).

Item 50 (I mainly use tests to gather information about students' learning.) is related to EFL teachers' skills in the use of varied assessment methods. In an examination-oriented culture, tests are a widely-used means that teachers use to measure student learning. Despite that assessment reform has been initiated in China for a few years, this remains to be the situation in most middle schools. Item 50 is an indirect statement intended to examine whether EFL teachers conform to the curriculum requirements and use a variety of assessment methods to assess student learning.

Item 32 (I take into account students' daily performance when marking.) is related to reliability in scoring. This is related but not contrary to Item 20 (I can be consistent in marking) in Dimension 3. Item 42 (When designing tests, I would write several test items beyond the scope of the syllabus to meet the needs of some top students.) relates itself to test fairness. This is contradictory with Item 55 (When designing assessment tasks, I will think about the alignment between assessment content and teaching objectives.). In addition to these items, there is one more negatively-worded item (Item 47: I award low scores as a punishment to those students who hold a negative attitude towards English learning), which is borrowed from D. L. Lin (2016), to examine whether EFL teachers are ethical in assessment practices.

Item 53 (I use assessments to make comparisons between students.) is concerned with the use of assessment results. Making comparisons between students is the primary purpose of norm-referenced tests. Teacher-made assessments, however, are criterion-referenced, and the major purpose is to measure the extent to which the students have mastered what they have been learning. Therefore, this item is developed to measure EFL teachers' understanding of consequential validity.

In addition to these reverse questions, there are indirect items in the questionnaire to measure the constructs. These indirect items address how EFL teachers translate their assessment skills to classroom assessment practices and how they give considerations to critical issues in assessment, i. e. reliability, validity, fairness, and ethics. As mentioned previously, indirect items are used to target constructs in Dimension 5 in that EFL teachers are not familiar with these abstract assessment terms. It does not make much sense, for instance, to ask them directly how to make tests reliable or valid. With regards to the indirect items in Dimension 3, they are mainly designed to examine whether EFL teachers could/would translate what they are able to do in actual classroom assessments. Simply put, the items in Dimension 3 measure not only EFL teachers' technical skills in assessment, but also their actual doing in assessment practices.

The items in Dimension 4 are also indirect statements, addressing whether and to what extent EFL teachers take into account students' cognitive and affective characteristics in teaching and assessment. In addition to these essential items, some seemingly peripheral items are also included in this subscale (e. g. Item 44: I give mild criticism to those students who do not perform well on language assessments.) to make the initial pool broader and more comprehensive than the theoretical view of the construct (Clark & Watson, 1995).

5.2.3 Layout of the questionnaire

The questionnaire consists of four parts: the title, instructions, questionnaire items, and personal information. For the title, "assessment-related knowledge and skills" is used instead of the technical term LAL "to provide the respondents with initial orientation and to activate relevant background knowledge and content expectations" (Dörnyei & Taguchi, 2010, p. 18). The title is followed by instructions, which are of two types: general and specific. The general instructions cover the survey purpose, the time needed to complete the questionnaire items, the need for respondents to give honest answers, and a "thank you". Given that many EFL teachers might have a mistaken conception that assessment is basically identical with tests, additional instructions are given, explaining the scope of the term assessment in the survey. The specific instructions explain the domain of questions and how respondents should go about answering the questions.

After the instructions comes the central part of the questionnaire. Based on feedback from expert review and piloting, items are somewhat randomly organized but those with similar syntactic structures are grouped together given the length and complexity of the survey. This process divides the major part of the questionnaire into three sections, each with its own instructions. In so doing, respondents would not become confused and impatient by switching between different syntactic structures across different items, and would be able to complete the survey more efficiently (Kremmel & Harding, 2020).

A five-point Likert scale is used for the items in the survey. Different terms are used to represent the continuum of the scale for different types of items. Specifically, "unknowledgeable" and "extremely knowledgeable" are utilized to represent the poles of the scale for items addressing EFL teachers' assessment-related knowledge (i. e. items targeting Dimension 1 and 2); "very untrue of me" to "very true of me" are employed to indicate the extreme ends of the scale for items targeting EFL teachers' technical skills and their practices in teaching and assessment. Still, minor differences exist in the scale for these items. "Not sure" is used as the median point in the scale when the items are intended to measure teachers' technical skills in assessment, whereas the lengthy wording "sometimes untrue and sometimes true of me" is employed for the remainder.

The final part of the questionnaire focuses on respondents' background information, including the region in which the respondent works, gender, years of teaching, assessment training, highest academic degree, grade levels of teaching, geographic area of the school (rural, county town, urban), and the factors that affect their assessment practices. The inclusion of these factors is based primarily on the existent literature of mediating factors of AL that is reviewed in Section 2. 2. 3. The next section proceeds to a description of how the survey is administered online to gather evidence concerning the psychometric properties of the questionnaire.

5.3 Preliminary Validation of the Questionnaire

This section aims to establish preliminary construct validity of the LAL questionnaire. To this end, a large-scale survey was launched online to gather empirical data from Chinese EFL teachers at primary and middle (junior and senior) schools. EFA was performed to analyze the factor structure of the items in the survey. After the identification of the factors, the psychometric properties of the scale and subscales were investigated to lend support to the solution.

5.3.1 Administration of the survey online

The final version of the questionnaire (Appendix Ⅱ) was translated into Chinese and launched online in July 2020 (https://www. wjx. cn/jq/ 85736447. aspx). Both convenience sampling and snowball sampling were used to recruit a large number of respondents. The author first invited her teachers, friends, former classmates and students to participate in the survey, then requested them to forward the invitation to others within their networks through social media Apps (QQ or WeChat). Among those that shared the survey link, some were principals or leaders in the local educational divisions, some were connected to the leaders in local educational departments or the personnel responsible for teacher training programs. Bonuses were set for some respondent groups via WeChat or QQ red envelops to increase respondents' interest in the survey. Due to these reasons, a large number of EFL teachers participated in the survey within three weeks, which was relatively a short period of time for survey research.

The data were exported from wjx. cn in August 2020. The exported data showed that 835 surveys had been started. Given the nature of online survey responses, a relatively conservative approach was taken to clean the data, removing: (1) any survey that was completed in less than 240 seconds; (2) any survey where the respondent gave identical answers to all the items; (3) any survey that had a string of identical answers to ten and more consecutive items; and (4) any survey that had a mean value greater than 4. 5 or lower than 1. 5. This process resulted in a final sample of $n=439$.

Table 5-3 displays the demographic characteristics of the 439 respondents that provided valid responses to the survey items. Of these EFL teachers, 55 (12. 5%) are male and 384 (87. 5%) are female. Given the gender distribution of the EFL teacher population in China, such a proportion is acceptable. In terms of the provinces they come from, 254 respondents (53. 2%) are from 14 different areas (including one self-administrative zone) in Hunan province; 173 teachers (39. 4%) come from 5 different areas in Guangdong province, i. e. Zaoqing, Jiangmen, Guangzhou, Shenzhen, and Foshan. The remaining 12 respondents are from eight other provinces or municipality directly under the central government (Anhui, Fujian,

Gansu, Guangxi, Hubei, Jiangxi, Shandong, and Shanghai).

Table 5-3 Demographic Characteristics of Respondents

Demographics	Characteristics	Frequency	Percent
Gender	Male	55	12.5
	Female	384	87.5
Province	Hunan (14 geographic areas)	254	57.9
	Guangdong (5 geographic areas)	173	39.4
	Others	12	2.7
Years of teaching	Less than 5 years	77	17.5
	5~10 years	68	15.5
	11~15 years	69	15.7
	16~20 years	89	20.3
	More than 20 years	136	31.0
Assessment training	Yes	288	65.6
	No	151	34.4
Highest level of academic degree	Associate degree	29	6.6
	Bachelor	370	84.3
	Master	39	8.9
	Others	1	0.2
Grade level	Primary school	98	22.3
	Junior middle school	215	49.0
	Senior middle school	126	28.7
Geographic area of the school	Rural	188	42.8
	County town	164	37.4
	Urban	87	19.8

With respect to years of teaching, 77 respondents (17.5%) have a teaching experience less than 5 years, 68 EFL teachers (15.5%) have a teaching experience of 5 ~ 10 years, 69 teachers (15.7%) have been teaching for 11~15 years, 89 teachers (20.3%) for 16~20 years, and 136 EFL teachers (31.0%) for more than 20 years. These teachers also differ in terms of assessment-related training experiences. Two hundred and eighty-eight teachers (65.5%) have received some amount of training in educational assessment in general or language assessment in particular, while 151 respondents (34.4%) have received no assessment-related training. In terms of the highest academic degree they obtain, 29 teachers (6.6%) have an associate degree, 370 teachers (84.3%) have a bachelor's degree, 39 teachers (8.9%) obtain a master's degree, and 1 teacher (0.2%) has other kind of degree.

As for the grade levels the respondents teach, 98 teachers (22.3%) work at primary schools, 215 teachers (49.0%) at junior middle schools, and 126 EFL teachers (28.7%) at senior middle schools. In terms of the geographic area of the school, 188 respondents (42.8%) work in schools in the rural areas, 164 teachers (37.4%) work in schools in county towns, and 87 EFL teachers (19.8%) in urban schools.

To sum up, the statistics of respondents' demographic information displayed in Table 5-3 demonstrate that the participant teachers are representative of the target EFL teacher population, except for the fact that they are mainly from two provinces.

5.3.2 Psychometric properties of the questionnaire

All the statistical analyses were performed on SPSS (Version 25.0). A preliminary reliability analysis showed a coefficient alpha of .942, suggesting that the questionnaire was an excellent instrument for measuring the intended constructs.

5.3.2.1 Exploratory factor analysis of items in the survey

In social science studies, EFA is often employed to discover complex patterns in a set of variables by examining the dataset and testing predictions (Child, 2006), and it is normally the initial step in constructing scales (Yong & Pearce, 2013). In Section 5.1, a five-factor structure was detected for the questionnaire items. Hence in this part, EFA was used to examine whether such a factor structure held in the respondents' responses, and to explore ways to reduce the questionnaire to a feasible instrument for future research and use.

Before EFA was conducted, the dataset was inspected to make sure that it met the assumptions for factor analysis. First, inter-item and item-total correlations were checked. Inspection of an initial correlation matrix of all items (the table omitted) showed that the vast majority of correlation values were close to .30, except for Item 37, 44, 47, and 50, which might suggest their removal from factor analysis. Item-total correlations are an index of discrimination. Generally, the acceptable value is set above .3, and the higher the discrimination indicator, the better the item is able to separate respondents according to their level located on the measurement scale (Wu & Adams, 2007). Item-total correlation statistics indicated that Item 47, a reverse question, had a negative value, suggesting that responses to this item needed to be reversely coded. All the other negative or seemingly reverse questions were positively correlated with the total scores, suggesting the assessment practices as described in these items were not uncommon with EFL teachers. Thus, responses to these items were not transformed. It merits our attention that the value of item-total correlations was quite low with Item 37 (.021, after transformation), Item 44 (.177), Item 47 (.036), and Item 50 (.118). A trial removal of the items with low discrimination slightly enhanced the reliability of the overall questionnaire (the table omitted). Due to the low inter-item and item-total correlations with Item 37, 44, 47, and 50, these four items were removed from the subsequent EFA.

Second, the sample size was adequate with respect to the recommended size of a minimum of 300 for factor analysis in the literature (Comrey & H. B. Lee, 1992) and relatively satisfactory in terms of item-to-participant ratio (approximately 1 : 7.5) given the large number of items in the questionnaire (see Loewen & Gonulal, 2015).

Third, the Kaiser-Meyer-Olkin (KMO) Measure of Sampling

Adequacy and Bartlett's test of sphericity were checked. The KMO measure of sampling adequacy was .942, far above .7, the acceptable level in literature. As such, the evidence suggested that the sample size was adequate to yield distinct and reliable factors. Bartlett's test of sphericity showed that Chi-square (1653) was 10868.631 (p<.001), indicating that the correlations between items were relatively compact and factor analysis would yield distinct and reliable factors.

EFA was conducted with principal axis factoring as opposed to principal components analysis because the primary purpose was to detect the latent constructs underlying response patterns, not to apply factor analysis for data reduction. The extracted communalities of the 58 items ranged from .209 to .647 (the table omitted), with a mean of .487. In terms of rotation, a direct oblimin rotation (an oblique rotation) was chosen over varimax (an orthogonal rotation) because relatively high correlations were expected between the latent constructs, given that expertise in language assessment might develop in related ways across the dimensions. For a simple display format, the coefficients of items were sorted by size and suppressed with factor loadings set at .40.

Given that the interpretation of factor analysis is based on many factors (e. g. rotated factor loadings, rotated eigenvalues, and scree test), more than one extraction technique was used to obtain the most parsimonious factor structure. The first run of EFA was performed by employing the rule of thumb—Kaiser's criterion—to extract factors with eigenvalues greater than one (Kaiser, 1960, cited from Cliff, 1988), and it resulted in 12 distinct factors (the table omitted). The overestimation in the number of factors extracted has long been considered as the major weakness of this rule of thumb (Child, 2006; Costello & Osborne, 2005), especially when there are more than 50 variables (Wu, 2010). Removing factors that had less than 3 items (Yong & Pearce, 2013) and items that cross-loaded on two or more factors, the results suggested a 5-factor solution.

Some researchers (e. g. Yong & Pearce, 2013) suggest the use of the scree test in conjunction with the eigenvalues to determine the optimum number of factors. As shown in Figure 5-2 below, the scree plot suggested a maximum of five factors to be extracted as indicated by the point where the curve straightened out (Child, 2006). Wu (2010) argues that factors with eigenvalues greater than 1 need to be taken into account in factor analysis. Therefore, more runs of EFA were performed by extracting 5, 6, 7, 8, 9, 10, 11, and 12 factors respectively. The results indicated that when extracting five or six factors, there were only three or four factors to be retained respectively, and some of the factors were difficult to interpret. However, a 5-factor solution held when extracting 7 to 12 factors. Additionally, the factors included fairly similar items in these different runs of analyses and the Cronbach α for each factor was also satisfactory. More importantly, the factor structure was rather similar to that identified in the second piloting (see Table 5-1). ① The stability of the factor structure and its consistency with the five dimensions of LAL model on which the questionnaire was built served as solid evidence of the construct validity of the questionnaire.

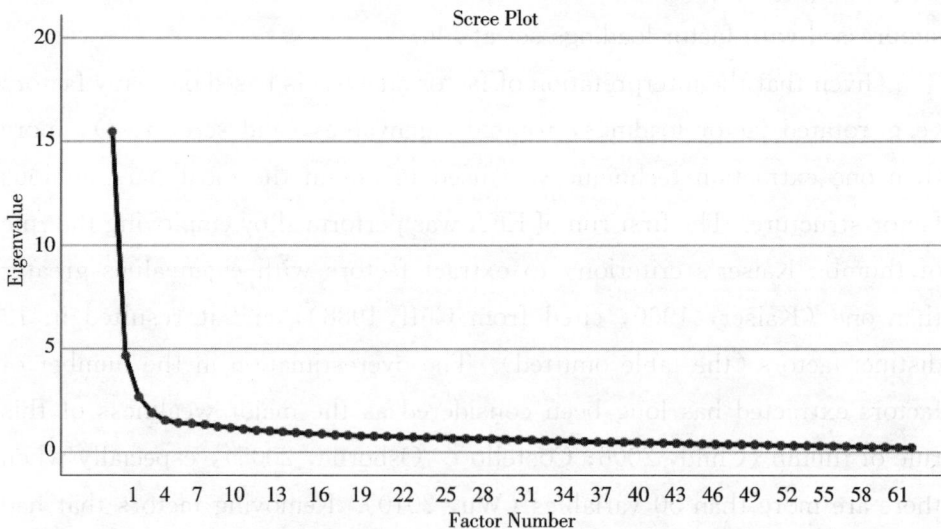

Figure 5-2   Scree Plot of EFA with 58 Items

---

① The numbering of items in the main study was different from that in the second piloting.

In terms of the resultant factor structure identified with different extractions, the analysis produced the most parsimonious and reliable pattern matrix when 7 factors were extracted. Consequently, the final version of the survey was obtained by removing items not included in the pattern matrix identified in this run of analysis. Removing factors that had less than 3 items (Yong & Pearce, 2013) and items that cross-loaded on two or more factors, the outcome was the removal of 18 items, leaving a final collection of 40 items for the measuring instrument (Appendix Ⅲ).

The eigenvalues were shown in Table 5-4. From the table, we can see the 5-factor solution explained 38.882% of the total variance in responses after rotation. Following the analysis, the items that loaded onto the identified factors were scrutinized to identify their commonalities and to develop labels for each of the five dimensions.

Table 5-4   Eigenvalues for the 5-factor Solution

Factor	Initial Eigenvalues			Extraction Sums of Squared Loadings		
	Total	% of Variance	Cumulative %	Total	% of Variance	Cumulative %
1	15.432	26.607	26.607	14.887	25.668	25.668
2	4.596	7.925	34.532	4.057	6.995	32.663
3	2.591	4.468	39.000	2.018	3.480	36.143
4	1.411	2.433	41.433	.823	1.419	37.562
5	1.311	2.260	43.693	.766	1.320	38.882

Factor 1 included three items related to incorporating students' cognitive and affective characteristics in foreign language teaching and assessment, and this factor was thus labeled as awareness of students' cognitive and affective characteristics. There were 11 items in Factor 2, eight of which were related to the use of assessments in teaching and learning contexts and three items were related to language teaching. This factor was labeled assessment in language pedagogy. Factor 3 also included 11 items, each of which was initially hypothesized to be related to the various processes of assessment. This factor was thus identified with the same label—technical skills in assessment. Factor 4 contained 8 items which were initially hypothesized to be related to awareness of assessment principles & ethic considerations in assessment practices. This factor was thus identified as originally labeled—assessment principles & ethic considerations. Factor 5 included 7 items, four of which were related to knowledge of language and language abilities; the other three items were related to knowledge of the *National English Curriculum Standards*, the CSE, and the influence of Chinese on English learning. This factor was labeled as knowledge of linguistics and applied linguistics. Overall, the extracted factors and the items included in each factor were consistent with the LAL conceptualization, lending support to the construct validity of the questionnaire.

5.3.2.2   Reliability and correlational analysis

With the factor structure of the questionnaire identified, the next step in EFA was to investigate the reliability of the overall scale and the correlations between the factors. Cronbach's coefficient α was calculated for each subscale to determine the internal consistency of items within each factor.

The results showed that the five subscales had a reliability coefficient of .747, .884, .902, .813, and .852 respectively. The highest coefficient went to the subscale of technical skills in assessment, and the lowest to the subscale of awareness of students' cognitive and affective characteristics. The reliability estimate of the overall scale was .939, indicating that the questionnaire was a superb instrument for examining the intended construct (Davies, 1990). When we deleted one item at a time, the resultant coefficients ranged from .936 to .939, indicating no improvement in the overall α could be obtained by omitting any item from the scale. These reliability estimates showed that all the 40 items measured the EFL teachers' LAL levels consistently. The item-total statistics indicated that the discrimination indexes of these items ranged from .315 to .589 (the table omitted).

Table 5-5 displays the inter-factor correlation matrix. From this table, we can see there were weak to medium but significant correlations between the factors at the . 01 level, with the coefficients ranging from . 215 to . 605. These significant correlations suggest that EFL teachers develop different aspects of LAL in related ways. The highest correlation (. 605) was found between Factor 2 and Factor 5, indicating significant moderate correlation between EFL teachers' knowledge of assessment in language pedagogy and their knowledge of linguistics and applied linguistics.

Table 5-5   Factor Correlation Matrix

Factor	Factor 1	Factor 2	Factor 3	Factor 4	Factor 5
Factor 1	1. 00				
Factor 2	−. 220*	1. 00			
Factor 3	−. 450*	. 419*	1. 00		
Factor 4	. 511*	−. 258*	−. 445*	1. 00	
Factor 5	. 215*	. 605*	. 295*	−. 246*	1. 00

* Significant at the . 01 level (two-tailed)

5.4 Summary

This chapter provides a detailed account of how judgement and comments from domain experts and EFL teachers (pre- and in-service) informed the revision of the item pool. In the meantime, piloting the questionnaire in two stages provided further information for refining the survey. With the completion of the instrument, the questionnaire was administered online to gather EFL teachers' responses to the items in pursuit of evidence for its construct validity. EFA results suggested a reliable and distinct 5-factor solution to the factor structure of the items. Generally, the identified factors were consistent with the five dimensions in the LAL model proposed in Chapter 4, and they were found to have fairly good to satisfactory psychometric properties (i. e. reliability coefficients and inter-factor correlations). These indicators lent support to the construct validity of the questionnaire.

CHAPTER SIX
CHINESE EFL TEACHERS' LAL LEVELS

With the establishment of construct validity of the measuring instrument, this chapter aims to build on the empirical data collected from the survey to investigate the current LAL levels of Chinese primary and middle school EFL teachers. A double-level approach was employed for the finalised survey items (40 in total), whereby responses were first analyzed for the whole population of respondents' literacy in the five dimensions and then analyzed for different subgroups of EFL teachers. Subgroups were identified according to respondents' demographic information provided in the last part of the survey. EFL teachers were categorized according to the following criteria: the grade levels of teaching (primary school, junior middle school, or senior middle school), experiences of formal training in educational assessment and/or language assessment (trained or untrained), and the institutional context they work at (rural, county town, or urban). All the statistical analyses were conducted with SPSS (Version 25.0).

6.1　Descriptive Statistics of EFL Teachers' Self-reported LAL Levels

Descriptive statistics for each item were calculated to have a snapshot of EFL teachers' LAL levels. In the rating scale, 1 indicates "unknowledgeable" and 5 refers to "extremely knowledgeable" for Item 1 to

Item 19; yet for Item 20 to Item 62, 1 represents "very untrue of me" and 5 indicates "very true of me". 3 means "undecided" for Item 21 to Item 31, but "sometimes untrue and sometimes true of me" for Item 32 to Item 62. The statistics in Table 6-1 show that the mean value of the items ranged from 2. 89 (Item 18) to 4. 33 (Item 53), suggesting that the respondent teachers had different levels of literacy in different indicators of LAL. A closer look at these statistics shows that the respondents self-reported scores less than 3 on Item 3, 13, 15, 18 ("3" indicating "moderately knowledgeable") and scores greater than 4 on Item 21, 36, 38, 39, 53, 55, and 61 ("4" indicating "essentially true of me").

Table 6-1   Descriptive Statistics of EFL Teachers' Scores on Each Item

Item	Min	Max	Mean	s	Item	Min	Max	Mean	s
Item 1	1	5	3. 06	. 884	Item 22	2	5	3. 85	. 697
Item 2	1	5	3. 30	. 758	Item 23	1	5	3. 91	. 756
Item 3	1	5	2. 93	. 977	Item 24	1	5	3. 64	. 710
Item 4	1	5	3. 85	. 916	Item 25	1	5	3. 74	. 767
Item 5	1	5	3. 56	. 920	Item 26	1	5	3. 65	. 774
Item 6	1	5	3. 34	. 713	Item 27	1	5	3. 74	. 734
Item 7	1	5	3. 37	. 734	Item 28	2	5	3. 81	. 754
Item 8	1	5	3. 22	. 812	Item 29	1	5	3. 93	. 704
Item 9	1	5	3. 29	. 889	Item 30	2	5	3. 85	. 754
Item 10	1	5	3. 36	. 769	Item 36	1	5	4. 25	. 708
Item 11	1	5	3. 39	. 750	Item 38	1	5	4. 16	. 751
Item 12	1	5	3. 24	. 769	Item 39	2	5	4. 02	. 801
Item 13	1	5	2. 99	. 847	Item 53	1	5	4. 33	. 744
Item 14	1	5	3. 21	. 929	Item 55	2	5	4. 06	. 744
Item 15	1	5	2. 93	. 928	Item 57	1	5	3. 81	. 731
Item 17	1	5	3. 09	. 841	Item 58	2	5	3. 93	. 662
Item 18	1	5	2. 89	. 999	Item 59	1	5	3. 92	. 772
Item 19	1	5	3. 21	. 828	Item 60	1	5	3. 96	. 742
Item 20	2	5	3. 93	. 711	Item 61	2	5	4. 16	. 712
Item 21	2	5	4. 07	. 725	Item 62	1	5	3. 83	. 832

Specifically, the respondent EFL teachers lacked adequate knowledge of varied assessment methods (Item 3, mean = 2.93), peer- and self-assessment (Item 13, mean=2.99). They did not have much understanding of the structure of language (Item 15, mean=2.93) or the requirements of language abilities for students at their grade levels of teaching as described in the CSE (Item 18, mean=2.89). On the contrary, these EFL teachers demonstrated expertise in using specific and vivid teaching aids to assist English teaching (Item 39, mean = 4.02), encouraging students when providing feedback (Item 36, mean = 4.25), and motivating students to learn English (Item 38, mean=4.16). They could also articulate clearly the specific learning objectives of the unit they were teaching (Item 61, mean=4.16), describe language test results (Item 21, mean=4.07), give fair treatment to every student in assessment (Item 53, mean=4.33), and consider the alignment between assessment content and teaching objectives (Item 55, mean=4.06).

Factor analysis in Chapter 5 indicated that EFL teachers' LAL included five factors, and these factors corresponded to the five dimensions of the LAL model which the questionnaire was built on. Hence, in this section, EFL teachers' competence in each dimension and the overall scale was examined to have a full understanding of their current LAL levels. For the sake of clarity, participants' responses to the items in the same subscale (identified in EFA) were summed up to obtain a composite score.

Table 6-2 displays the descriptive statistics of EFL teachers' overall score and scores on the five dimensions. Given the variations in the number of items subsumed in different dimensions, the total possible, the minimum, and maximum scores are also provided in the table. From the table we can see EFL teachers' competence differed across the five dimensions, though they generally reported medium scores on each of the dimensions as well as on the overall scale as evidenced by the average scores. It is noteworthy that some EFL teachers obtained the highest possible score on F1, F3, F4, and almost the highest possible score on F5.

Table 6-2   Descriptive Statistics of EFL Teachers' Scores on Each Dimension①

Dimension	Total Possible	Min	Max	Mean	s
F1	15	6	15	12. 42	1. 84
F2	55	14	49	36. 06	6. 10
F3	55	23	55	42. 12	5. 75
F4	40	190	40	32. 00	3. 92
F5	35	9	34	22. 17	4. 61
Overall	200	90	186	144. 78	17. 21

Note: F1—awareness of students' cognitive and affective characteristics

F2—assessment in language pedagogy

F3—technical skills in assessment

F4—assessment principles & ethic considerations

F5—knowledge of linguistics and applied linguistics

For a more straightforward understanding of EFL teachers' self-reported literacy in each dimension, the average scores on each dimension and the overall scale were computed and transformed into a five-point Likert scale by dividing the number of items. The results are displayed in Table 6-3.

Table 6-3   Descriptive Statistics of EFL Teachers' Transformed Scores

Dimension	Min	Max	Mean	s
F1	2. 00	5. 00	4. 14	. 61
F2	1. 27	4. 45	3. 28	. 55
F3	2. 09	5. 00	3. 83	. 52
F4	2. 38	5. 00	4. 00	. 49
F5	1. 29	4. 86	3. 17	. 66
Overall	2. 25	4. 65	3. 62	. 43

---

① The factors identified in FA correspond to the five dimensions in the proposed LAL model. For the sake of conciseness, F1 to F5 are used to refer to the five different dimensions in this chapter.

As shown in the table above, EFL teachers reported medium levels of LAL as indicated by an average score of 3. 62. They received the highest score (4. 14) on F1 (awareness of students' cognitive and affective characteristics), and some EFL teachers obtained the maximum mean score of 5. 00. Among the three items in this subscale, i. e. Item 36, 38, and 39, EFL teachers received the highest mean on Item 36 (More often than not, I encourage students when I provide feedback to them about their performance on assessment tasks.). The second highest score was found on F4 (mean=4. 0, assessment principles & ethic considerations). Similar to F1, some EFL teachers obtained the maximum mean score of 5. 00. Among the eight items included in this dimension, EFL teachers scored highest on Item 53 (I give fair treatment to every student in assessment.), with a mean value of 4. 33.

Among the five dimensions, the lowest score (3. 17) was found on F5 (knowledge of linguistics and applied linguistics). The minimum score EFL teachers received on this subscale was 1. 29 (with a total score of 9 for 7 items), and the lowest item mean score on F5 (2. 89) went to Item 18, related to knowledge of the CSE. The EFL teachers also scored relatively low (3. 28) on F2 (assessment in language pedagogy), and some teachers obtained a minimum mean score of 1. 27. In this subscale, the participating teachers obtained the lowest mean (2. 99) on Item 3, which asked about EFL teachers' use of varied assessment methods. With regards to F3 (technical skills in assessment), the EFL teachers received a mean score of 3. 83, and some teachers received a maximum of 5. 00 on this dimension. EFL teachers' responses to F5 and F2 indicated that they had inadequate knowledge of learning theories, the CSE, methods of instruction, and approaches to assessment.

Taking a close look at Table 6-3, we could find great discrepancies in LAL levels among the participating EFL teachers. On one hand, there was a difference of .93 (4. 14—3. 17) in the average scores between the two dimensions of F1 and F5; on the other hand, some participants scored very or extremely high on some dimensions while a few other EFL teachers scored quite low on one or more dimensions as indicated by the low minimum mean score. Such findings are not unexpected, given differences among the EFL teachers in the highest academic degree, assessment training experiences, etc.

6.2   Comparison of EFL Teachers' LAL by Different Demographic Factors

One of the purposes of the current study is to investigate whether significant differences exist among EFL teachers in terms of different demographic characteristics. Parametric tests were chosen for statistical analysis. LAL differences among different groups of EFL teachers were examined for each dimension and the overall LAL.

6.2.1   Comparison of EFL teachers' LAL by grade levels of teaching

Table 6-4 displays the overall LAL scores and scores on each dimension for Chinese EFL teachers at different grade levels of teaching. As can be seen from this table, EFL teachers from primary schools, junior and senior middle schools self-reported approximate mean scores on each dimension except for F5. The differences in the overall literacy among the three groups of teachers were also slight.

For a direct comparison of EFL teachers' levels of literacy in different dimensions, each of the dimension scores was transformed into a five-point scale by dividing the number of items in the corresponding dimension. The results show EFL teachers at different grade levels of teaching demonstrated noticeably different literacy levels in F5 (knowledge of linguistics and applied linguistics), but they reported unexpectedly similar literacy levels in F1 (awareness of students' cognitive and affective characteristics), F2 (assessment in language pedagogy), F3 (technical skills in assessment), and F4 (assessment principles & ethic considerations).

Table 6-4   Descriptive Statistics of LAL Levels by Grade Levels of Teaching

Dimension	Grade levels	Mean	s	Std. Error
F1	Primary	4. 11	. 67	. 067
	Junior	4. 16	. 59	. 04
	Senior	4. 13	. 61	. 06
F2	Primary	3. 26	. 55	. 06
	Junior	3. 27	. 57	. 04
	Senior	3. 31	. 53	. 05
F3	Primary	3. 81	. 53	. 05
	Junior	3. 81	. 53	. 04
	Senior	3. 87	. 51	. 05
F4	Primary	3. 93	. 48	. 05
	Junior	4. 00	. 50	. 03
	Senior	4. 05	. 47	. 04
F5	Primary	2. 97	. 67	. 07
	Junior	3. 14	. 68	. 05
	Senior	3. 38	. 55	. 05
Overall	Primary	18. 07	2. 06	. 21
	Junior	18. 39	2. 21	. 15
	Senior	18. 73	2. 11	. 19

ANOVA test was performed to investigate whether significant differences existed among teachers from different grade levels of teaching. Table 6-5 showed that the differences were not significant for $F1(F(2)=.351)$, $F2(F(2)=.217)$, $F3(F(2)=.602)$, $F4(F(2)=1.679)$, and the overall scale $(F(2)=2.659)$ at the .05 level. However, significant difference was detected among EFL teachers in terms of literacy in F5, i. e. teachers at different grade levels of instruction demonstrated significantly different amounts of knowledge of linguistics and applied linguistics.

Table 6-5 ANOVA Test of LAL Levels by Grade Levels of Teaching

Dimension	Sum of squares	df	Mean square	F	Sig.
F1	.266	2	.133	.351	.704
F2	.134	2	.067	.217	.805
F3	.329	2	.165	.602	.548
F4	.802	2	.401	1.679	.188
F5	9.848	2	4.924	11.89*	.000
Overall	24.553	2	12.277	2.659	.071

* Significant at the .05 level (two-tailed)

Since the p-value was small for F5, post-hoc tests (LSD) were conducted to find out which pairs of groups differed significantly in literacy in F5. As shown in Table 6-6, there was significant difference in each group pair at the .05 level. EFL teachers at higher grade levels of teaching were more literate in F5 than those at lower grades of instruction. To be more specific, senior middle school EFL teachers reported significantly higher levels of knowledge of linguistics and applied linguistics than EFL teachers from primary and junior middle schools, and junior middle school EFL teachers also reported significantly better knowledge than primary EFL teachers.

Table 6-6 Post-hoc Tests of Differences in F5 by Grade Levels of Teaching

Group Pair	Mean Difference	Std. Error	Sig.
Primary-Junior	−.171*	.078	.030
Primary-Senior	−.414*	.087	.000
Junior-Senior	−.242*	.072	.001

* Significant at the .05 level.

6.2.2 Comparison of teachers' LAL by assessment training

Table 6-7 displays the descriptive LAL statistics of the two groups of

EFL teachers (trained vs. untrained) in the overall construct and the five dimensions representing the construct. A uniform tendency can be detected from the table: EFL teachers who had received assessment training reported higher scores on the subscales and the overall scale than those who had not.

Table 6-7   Descriptive Statistics of LAL Levels by Assessment Training

Dimension	Assessment training	Mean	s
F1	Yes	4. 17	. 612
	No	4. 09	. 618
F2	Yes	3. 39	. 503
	No	3. 07	. 591
F3	Yes	3. 88	. 490
	No	3. 74	. 569
F4	Yes	4. 04	. 446
	No	3. 93	. 559
F5	Yes	3. 29	. 634
	No	2. 94	. 648
Total	Yes	18. 76	2. 025
	No	17. 76	2. 254

Independent t-test was conducted to investigate whether such differences were statistically significant. The results are shown in Table 6-8. Overall, significant differences were detected between EFL teachers who had received assessment training and those who had not. When it comes to the different dimensions of LAL, the two groups of teachers self-reported similar scores on F1 (awareness of students' cognitive and affective characteristics), but they demonstrated significant differences in F2 (assessment in language pedagogy), F3 (technical skills in assessment), F4 (assessment principles & ethic considerations), and F5 (knowledge of linguistics and applied linguistics) at the . 05 level.

Table 6-8   t-test of EFL Teachers' Literacy Levels by Assessment Training

Dimension	t	df	Sig. (2-tailed)	Mean Difference	Std. Error Difference	95% Confidence Interval of the Difference	
						Lower	Upper
F1	1. 344	437	. 180	. 083	. 062	−. 038	. 204
F2	5. 905	437	. 000	. 317	. 054	. 212	. 422
F3	2. 740	437	. 006	. 143	. 052	. 040	. 245
F4	2. 147	437	. 032	. 105	. 049	. 009	. 201
F5	5. 394	437	. 000	. 346	. 064	. 220	. 472
Total	4. 697	437	. 000	. 994	. 212	. 578	1. 410

(t-test for Equality of Means)

* Significant at the . 05 level (two-tailed)

6.2.3 Comparison of teachers' LAL by institutional context

Table 6-9 displays the descriptive statistics of EFL teachers' literacy levels in the overall construct as well as the five dimensions representing the construct in terms of different institutional contexts. Generally, EFL teachers from rural, county town, and urban schools self-reported similar scores on the overall scale and four of the five dimensions. Yet, noticeable differences could be observed in the mean scores on F5 (knowledge of linguistics and applied linguistics).

Table 6-10 shows the ANOVA test results of teachers' LAL in terms of the institutional context. The statistics indicated that the differences were not significant for F1, F2, F3, F4, and the total scores (p>. 05). However, there were significant differences among EFL teachers in F5 (p<. 05), i. e. EFL teachers from rural, county town, and urban schools reported significantly different levels of knowledge of linguistics and applied linguistics.

Table 6-9 Descriptive Statistics of LAL Levels by Institutional Context

Dimension	Institutional Context	Mean	s	Std. Error
F1	Rural	4.13	.637	.046
	County town	4.15	.581	.045
	Urban	4.14	.634	.068
F2	Rural	3.22	.575	.042
	County town	3.30	.565	.044
	Urban	3.37	.477	.051
F3	Rural	3.81	.547	.040
	County town	3.83	.488	.038
	Urban	3.86	.536	.057
F4	Rural	3.98	.486	.035
	County town	3.98	.490	.038
	Urban	4.10	.488	.052
F5	Rural	3.06	.682	.050
	County town	3.25	.618	.048
	Urban	3.25	.655	.070
Total	Rural	18.19	2.195	.160
	County town	18.51	2.127	.166
	Urban	18.72	2.102	.225

Table 6-10 ANOVA Test of LAL Levels by Institutional Context

Dimension	Sum of squares	df	Mean square	F	Sig.
F1	.063	2	.032	.083	.920
F2	1.365	2	.683	2.229	.109
F3	.122	2	.061	.223	.800
F4	1.123	2	.561	2.357	.096
F5	4.135	2	2.068	4.842*	.008
Total	18.841	2	9.421	2.035	.132

* Significant at the .05 level (two-tailed)

To find out which pairs of groups differed significantly in F5, post-hoc test (LSD) was performed and the results were shown in Table 6-11. The table shows that significant difference ($p <. 05$) existed between EFL teachers from rural schools and those working in schools in county towns and urban areas. Specifically, EFL teachers in county town and urban schools self-reported significantly higher scores than their counterparts in rural schools. However, no significant difference was detected with EFL teachers working at county town and urban schools ($p >. 05$).

Table 6-11   Post-hoc Tests of Differences in F5 by Institutional Context

Sample 1～Sample 2	Mean Difference	Std. Error	Sig.
Rural-County town	$-. 198^*$	. 070	. 005
Rural-Urban	$-. 192^*$	. 085	. 024
County town-Urban	. 006	. 087	. 949

* Significant at the . 05 level.

6.3 Summary

In this chapter, Chinese EFL teachers' current LAL levels were investigated based on the empirical data gathered through the formal survey. Generally, the participating EFL teachers reported basic levels of LAL, and they demonstrated different levels of literacy in different dimensions. They were more aware of students' cognitive and affective characteristics in teaching and assessment, generally followed assessment principles, and took into account ethic issues in assessment practices. Relatively speaking, EFL teachers reported lower levels of knowledge in terms of assessment in language pedagogy and linguistics and applied linguistics. Their literacy levels in technical skills in language assessment ran somewhere between basic and adequate.

The respondent EFL teachers also showed significant differences in LAL in terms of different demographic characteristics. First, EFL teachers from different grade levels of teaching differed significantly in terms of knowledge of linguistics and applied linguistics. Teachers from senior middle schools reported significantly higher levels of knowledge of linguistics and applied linguistics than teachers from primary schools and junior middle schools, and junior middle school EFL teachers also reported higher levels of knowledge of linguistics and applied linguistics than primary EFL teachers. Second, assessment training experiences exerted significant influence on EFL teachers' overall LAL. Teachers who had received training in language assessment or assessment in general education reported higher levels of literacy than those who had not. Yet, the participating EFL teachers demonstrated comparable awareness of students' cognitive and affective characteristics in teaching and assessment and assessment principles & ethic considerations in assessment practices. Third, the geographic area of the school the teacher works at is also a significant factor to consider in the investigation of EFL teachers' knowledge of linguistics and applied linguistics. EFL teachers from urban and county town schools reported higher levels of knowledge than primary EFL teachers, but the difference between urban teachers and teachers in county town schools was not significant.

CHAPTER SEVEN
DISCUSSION AND IMPLICATIONS

7.1 Discussion

The present research aims to address Chinese primary and middle school EFL teachers' LAL. To this end, the research attempts to seek answers to three research questions revolving around the "what", "how", and "to what degree" of the EFL teachers' LAL. This section discusses the research findings in sequence.

7.1.1 The LAL construct for Chinese EFL teachers

The first research question is "what assessment knowledge and skills do Chinese EFL teachers need in order to assess students effectively?". An attempt was made to analyze what type of assessment knowledge and skills teachers of all subject areas needed to possess to be effective teacher assessors through document and thematic analyses of different professional standards for teachers, prominent assessment standards, and a review of research studies of AL in general education. Then LAL studies were reviewed for the unique components that EFL teachers needed for sound assessments. On the basis of detailed analyses, the LAL construct for Chinese EFL teachers was defined as "a set of knowledge, skills, and principles that EFL teachers need in order to assess effectively students' language learning in relation to the learning objectives, language use abilities, and capacity for language learning, and to provide immediate, appropriate, and useful feedback to them". Specifically, an assessment literate EFL teacher:

(1) is familiar with language learning objectives against which to assess students;

(2) is familiar with the various components of language knowledge and ability and understands how these components are developed;

(3) is aware of students' cognitive and affective characteristics in language teaching and assessment;

(4) understands student' language learning processes and their capacity for language learning;

(5) is familiar with assessment processes and different assessment methods;

(6) is aware of the principles and ethic considerations that guide language assessments;

(7) is skilled in choosing, designing, and scoring classroom language assessments and communicating assessment results appropriately to pupils and their parents;

(8) gets students to involve in assessments;

(9) assesses effectively students' language learning outcomes and gives them a sense of progression;

(10) provides timely and useful feedback to students; and

(11) makes evidence-informed adjustments in instruction and facilitates students' learning.

Noticeably, this comprehensive definition has drawn considerably from AL related literature and research, but it distinguishes itself from AL with an inclusion of "unique aspects inherent in theorizing and assessing language-related performance" (Inbar-Lourie, 2017, p. 259). Understandings of what is prerequisite for effective language assessors and the depth of the knowledge needed are dependent on the assessment context. China is an examination-oriented culture, with language assessment having its roots in the testing tradition. Though assessment reforms have been initiated in recent years, a more comprehensive assessment framework which integrates assessment with learning is yet to be established. Therefore, considerable emphasis is placed on the testing aspects in the LAL definition.

The definition above incorporates the latest developments in language learning and assessment theories. J. Y. Lee (2019) emphasizes the role of learning in conceptualizing LAL, arguing that EFL teachers' understanding of language learning and teaching principles is a central and unique characteristic of LAL. In the meantime, learners voice their concerns about the affective and cognitive elements in assessments (Butler *et al.*, 2021). They tend to be greatly affected by assessment experiences (either positive or negative) and their teachers' attitudes towards assessment (Butler, 2019; Butler *et al.*, 2021; Carless & Lam, 2014). To improve their experiences with assessment, EFL teachers need to take heed of young learners' vulnerability when designing assessments (Butler, 2019).

In the follow-up questionnaire, when asked about their understanding of students' cognitive and affective characteristics, 13.64% of the respondent EFL teachers reported little understanding, 50% of teachers reported a basic understanding, 31.82% of teachers chose fairly good understanding, and another 4.55% of teachers selected quite good understanding. A majority of these teachers often (42.11%) or always (26.32%) gave thought to students' cognitive and affective characteristics when designing teaching or assessment activities, 28.95% of these teachers did this sometimes, and 2.63% of teachers occasionally did this. Incorporating learners' cognitive and affective characteristics in LAL is aligned with the learner-centered approach to learning, reflective of the latest developments in assessment and AL theories. It also reflects practising EFL teachers' assessment practices.

Different from most previous LAL conceptualizations, this definition gives due attention to the characteristics of an educational setting where English is learned as a foreign language and seldom used outside the classroom. Data from the follow-up survey showed 86.36% of the EFL teachers reported that they often needed to motivate students to learn English, and 11.36% of the teachers needed to motivate students sometimes. The data also suggested various reasons for students' lack of motivation, and the most important one was students' weakness in the English subject, which resulted in their low interest in English learning. Other reasons included boring teaching and unauthentic teaching content, the way they were assessed (testing has been the primary means of assessment and students get frustrated easily), and difficulty in learning due to great differences in pronunciation and grammar between the English and Chinese languages. To develop and maintain students' interest in English learning, EFL teachers need to give students a sense of progression.

In line with the comprehensive definition, an LAL model was developed to show the body of assessment knowledge and skills prerequisite for Chinese EFL teachers. This model is framed within Davies' (2008) "skills+knowledge+principles" approach, which is dominant in theoretical and empirical research of LAL (Giraldo, 2018). There are five dimensions underlying the three components. Specifically, the knowledge component includes knowledge of assessment in language pedagogy, knowledge of linguistics and applied linguistics, and awareness of students' cognitive and affective characteristics. The skills component refers to the technical skills involved in the various assessment processes, ranging from selecting/developing sound assessments to reporting assessment results to students and other stakeholders. The principles component indicates assessment principles & ethic considerations in assessment practices. These elements are deemed as a necessary condition for EFL teachers to be able to function professionally in classroom assessment of students' language performances.

Due to the complex nature of the LAL construct, what makes the focal elements of a conceptual LAL framework remains controversial (Inbar-Lourie, 2017). Despite a general consensus on the "knowledge + skills + principles" approach to LAL, researchers have different understandings of the importance of these elements. Inbar-Lourie (2008b) underscored the assessment context and the consequences of language assessment as core LAL concepts, while Fulcher (2012) conceptualized LAL as consisting of understanding of assessment context, principles, and practices. The LAL model proposed in this study shares many focal components with previous models in assessment literature (Davies, 2008; Kremmel & Harding, 2020; Pan, 2020; Taylor, 2013), underscoring the socially constructed and contextually specific nature of assessment practices (Inbar-Lourie, 2008b). It is also reflective of the current educational assessment landscape and incorporates the latest developments in AL and LAL theories.

With the prevalence of standards-based education reform in China and in the globe, assessment is used not just as a means of measuring students' learning, but more of a tool to move students forward toward learning outcomes. To be competent in language assessment, EFL teachers need to acquire a solid understanding of the English language so that they are comfortable when integrating assessment in instruction. In the meantime, they need to possess basic understandings of linguistics and applied linguistics and research findings in these fields. Only equipped with such a body of knowledge can EFL teachers be clear about what aspects of language to assess students (what to assess), the various purposes for which assessments are conducted (why assess), and the different methods they can use to achieve their purposes (how to assess). In addition, EFL teachers need to know the different types of language assessments and be aware of the assessment principles and ethics in assessments.

Framed within Davies' "skills + knowledge + principles" approach to

LAL, the present model distinguishes itself from previous ones for its inclusion of awareness of students' cognitive and affective characteristics for observed assessment practices and a focus on the learner and the learning process. The expertise required to conduct sound classroom assessments is contingent on a multitude of factors, ranging from the resources available to the individual learning needs of students, and the most important one is the student factor. Recently, there is an emphasis on a learner-centered approach to language education (Lambert *et al.*, 2017) wherein student needs are reflected in curriculum, teaching, and assessment to motivate and help them become autonomous learners (Butler *et al.*, 2021). In the field of assessment, assessment for learning is highly valued (Black & Wiliam, 1998; Colby-Kelly & Turner, 2007; Brookhart, 2011), and learners are considered as important stakeholders in assessment (e.g. Kremmel & Harding, 2020). There is a growing focus on the learners' perspectives in assessment studies (e.g. Butler, 2018; Butler & J. Y. Lee, 2010; Winke & Goertler, 2008) and validation research (Cheng & DeLuca, 2011). Recent research also takes into account young learners' perspectives in LAL discussions (Butler *et al.*, 2021). Considering the centrality of learners and their needs in education and assessment, we need to incorporate students' cognitive and affective characteristics when unpacking the set of knowledge EFL teachers need in order to perform assessment-related tasks.

    Students learn English as a foreign language in a Chinese educational setting. With limited exposure to language interaction, learners take a path in learning the foreign language different from that taken when acquiring the mother tongue or a second language. EFL teachers need to adopt English teaching strategies that are effective in an EFL context so that learners could feel less pressure in learning the language. Additionally, learners at the stage of basic education are in a state of flux. They are developing physically, emotionally, and cognitively (McKay, 2006). A clear understanding of students' age-related, cognitive, and affective characteristics at different stages will help EFL teachers choose assessment tasks and methods that conform to students' developmental characteristics and provide feedback in a way that will boost students' confidence in language learning.

The inclusion of awareness of students' cognitive and affective characteristics also highlights the context-dependent and cultural-specific nature of classroom language assessments in a Chinese educational context, where classroom is the locus in which students learn the language. The context-dependent and cultural-specific nature of classroom assessments requires that assessment practices be student-centered and motivation-oriented. On one hand, the purpose of classroom assessment is to facilitate student learning. To assess students effectively, EFL teachers need to incorporate learners' current language development as well as their cognitive, affective factors in the design and implementation of foreign language assessment tasks. It is also important for EFL teachers to encourage students to be significant users of assessment information to support and monitor their own learning. While teachers are required to use assessment information to facilitate data-driven decisions for instructional purposes, an emphasis on assessment literacy also requires teachers to understand how assessment can be used pedagogically as a learning tool for students. In the meantime, students are also agents of assessment. Student-led assessment is more than an act of receiving a grade from a peer or giving oneself a grade. Through self- and peer-assessment, students internalize criteria for success, make judgement about their learning, and develop the capacity to support and monitor subsequently their learning in relation to these criteria.

On the other hand, the difficulty in learning a foreign language in a context where it is seldom used outside the classroom is well established in literature. Students differ in language development, cognitive and affective characteristics. These factors in combination require that, at the stage of basic education, foreign language assessment should be in line with the cognitive and affective characteristics of the students (McKay, 2006). A case in point is that most English textbooks for primary students include assessment activities in the form of games and songs. The fun elements in assessment tasks aim to stimulate students' interest in English and motivate them to learn the language. EFL teachers design tasks in such a way that assessment results give learners (especially young learners) a sense of progression(ibid). When providing feedback to students, EFL teachers pay heed to learners' confidence in language learning and encourage them when students do not perform well.

LAL is a dynamic, complex construct. The body of assessment knowledge and skills Chinese EFL teachers need to perform assessment-related tasks tends to vary with the introduction of a new foreign language strategy and assessment-related reforms. The proposed LAL model is indicative of assessment policy initiatives in China and the contemporary assessment landscape in the globe by incorporating assessment for learning in its components. It also underscores the language element, making LAL an integrated construct. Different from previous models, this one is based on a comprehensive analysis of standards documents and research studies, and its validity is established through feedback from experienced EFL teachers and experts in the assessment community.

7.1.2　The LAL measuring instrument for Chinese EFL teachers

The second research question to be answered in this research is "what instrument can we use to assess Chinese EFL teachers' LAL levels?". Different instruments have been constructed to examine language teachers' LAL (e. g. Kremmel & Harding, 2020; Xu & Brown, 2017), but they are not appropriate for the purpose of the current research since LAL is susceptible to changes in contexts, policy, and culture (Xu & Brown, 2016). A new measuring instrument needs to be developed to better align with the Chinese assessment context and, in the meantime, to differentiate educational settings for the differential priorities at different stages of education.

The development of a measuring instrument is the most challenging in LAL research. For a solid foundation for its construction, it is prerequisite to understand the nature and extent of the components within the LAL constructs, especially the language component. The construction of the instrument also needs to be built upon recent professional standards and contemporary assessment policies in specific contexts and, meanwhile, reflective of recent developments in AL/LAL theories. In the current research, relevant studies and standards documents were reviewed to well represent the constructs in the measuring tool, and an initial pool of items was constructed. In the process of constructing these items, due attention was paid to China's educational context with reference to *China's English Curriculum Standards* for compulsory education and general high schools as well as Chinese researchers' academic work.

After the pooling of the initial items, experts were recruited to provide feedback on the items. Each expert rated on a five-point scale the extent to which the items were aligned with the LAL definition and theoretical model. Based on expert feedback, items were added, revised, and amended until all items met the validation criteria. In addition to expert feedback, the questionnaire also underwent two stages of piloting wherein both qualitative and quantitative feedback was collected to inform further revision.

Statistical analysis of the data gathered in the second piloting indicated that the measuring instrument had a reliability coefficient of .956 and a five-factor structure approximate to the dimensions of the proposed model. Yet, some items underwent further revision for their low discrimination. The final survey included a total of 62 items, addressing the dimensions in the preliminary LAL model with a differing number of items. It was launched online to gather EFL teachers' responses. Comparatively robust exploratory factor analysis of the cleaned data (i. e. removing items with low discrimination indexes and factor loadings) showed that the items had a five-factor structure approximate to that identified in the second piloting, which was consistent with the dimensions in the proposed model. This indicates that the questionnaire has desirable psychometric qualities and the constructs have "operational structural integrity" (Fulcher, 2012, p. 117). The validity of the instrument confirms the importance of developing a teacher LAL survey tool based upon more recent assessment standards (e. g. JCSEE, 2015) and contemporary assessment policies in Chinese educational context (Xu & Brown, 2017).

The questionnaire was empirically reduced to a more feasible instrument with 40 items. These items loaded onto five different factors. The five subscales had a coefficient α of . 747, . 884, . 902, . 813, and . 852 respectively, and the overall scale had a reliability coefficient of . 939. These indices suggest the questionnaire is a superb instrument for examining the intended construct. Nevertheless, more empirical research is needed for construct validation of the instrument with the use of more powerful statistical analysis (i. e. confirmatory factor analysis).

In the development of the measuring instrument, some items were borrowed from Kremmel and Harding's (2020) Language Assessment Literacy Survey (the Survey, for short). Yet, the measuring tool constructed in the research is much different from the Survey in Kremmel and Harding (2020) for its different theoretical underpinnings, research purpose, and the targeted population. Kremmel and Harding (2020) constructed the Survey with an aim to elaborate and validate Taylor's (2013) hypothetical LAL profiles for different stakeholders. This instrument was designed for use across different contexts and stakeholder groups. In this sense, Kremmel and Harding did not take into consideration the specific educational context in which assessment was implemented when designing the Survey. Different from this survey, the measuring instrument developed in this study is theoretically grounded on a hypothetical LAL model, which is built on research literature and standards documents of different kinds and from different countries and regions. It also takes account of the contextual nature of assessment with an inclusion of items that show the unique characteristics of foreign language learning in China's educational setting. By focusing on the EFL teacher population, the items in the tool address assessment competence most relevant to teachers' classroom assessment needs.

The development of an LAL measuring instrument is a complicated process. The time, resources, and expertise required in this undertaking present great challenges to researchers, and this accounts for the unavailability of "a grounded language assessment inventory" (Inbar-Lourie, 2013, p. 6) in the field. In this study, great efforts were made to construct an instrument to measure Chinese EFL teachers' LAL levels, and this tool was detected to be reliable and valid. The development of such a measuring tool distinguishes the present study from most previous studies for its different theoretical underpinnings.

Due to the researcher's limited sources, inadequate time and energy, there are admittedly inadequacies in the LAL conceptualization and the measuring instrument. Future studies may include cooperating with representatives of other disciplines (e. g. educational psychology researchers and domain experts) (Lan & Fan, 2019) and incorporating the perspectives of different stakeholders, especially the practising teachers, concerning the assessment expertise that they deem as necessary for good practice in language pedagogy (Xu & Brown, 2017). Additionally, close observations of EFL teachers' assessment practices will help identify whether and how progressive stages of LAL exist (ibid). Particularly, differentiating between competencies needed at different levels of instruction may help define LAL in a more effective way. These approaches will help establish solid LAL constructs and lay a solid foundation for the construction of an

LAL measure (Xu & Brown, 2017).

7.1.3 Chinese EFL teachers' LAL levels

The third research question is "what are Chinese EFL teachers' current LAL levels?", and it includes two subquestions:

(1) What is Chinese EFL teachers' overall literacy in language assessment and their expertise in each of the LAL dimensions?

(2) To what extent and in what ways are EFL teachers' demographic characteristics (i. e. grade levels of teaching, assessment training, and the institutional context) related to their different competences in identified LAL dimensions?

7.1.3.1 EFL teachers' overall LAL

In terms of overall literacy in language assessment, EFL teachers reported a basic level of LAL (a mean score of 3.62 on a five-point Likert scale), indicating insufficient expertise for them to be effective in classroom assessment. This finding was confirmed by data from the follow-up survey, which showed that 18.18% of the EFL teachers had rather good knowledge of assessment, 36.36% of the teachers had basic understanding, 40.91% of them knew a little about assessment, and another 4.55% of teachers basically lacked knowledge about assessment. This research finding is consistent with previous studies (Alkharusi et al., 2011; Boraie, 2015; Hasselgreen et al., 2004; Lam, 2019; Lan & Fan, 2019; D. L. Lin, 2016; Mertler, 2004; Nan, 2016; Plake et al., 1993; Xu & Brown, 2017; D. H. Zheng, 2010; D. H. Zheng & Ye, 2012).

Teachers' insufficient AL/LAL is a global concern. For Chinese EFL teachers, factors at the macro, meso, and micro levels may account for this. At the macro level, as argued by Xu and Brown (2017), there is a lack of assessment policies, professional standards and guidelines at various levels to guide teacher assessment practice and promote teacher AL.

Additionally, AL is not an indispensable part for teacher accreditation. Within this context, EFL teachers have no external directives and steering documents to evaluate and assure their assessment practices. At the meso level, the curriculum structure of initial teacher education programs, policies and supports from school leadership for assessment, the school's climate for supporting assessment practices, and school-wide access to tools and support around assessment are important factors that influence EFL teachers' LAL (ibid). Due to a lack of support from national documents, school leadership is unlikely to be aware of the pertinence of assessment in teaching and learning and to be supportive of EFL teachers' LAL development. At the micro level, EFL teachers' CoA and their willingness to enhance AL/LAL are also crucial. Data from the follow-up survey indicated that all the EFL teachers considered teaching and assessment to be closely related, and a vast majority of them deemed that assessment was a means to evaluate teaching effectiveness and the assessment results should be used to facilitate teaching. However, without guidance from national policies and documents and support from school leadership, it is difficult for EFL teachers to realize the pedagogical power of formative assessment in facilitating student learning and experience a need for change in their assessment expertise.

Despite EFL teachers' basic level of overall LAL, we are not in a position to extend this claim to the different dimensions representing LAL. EFL teachers were identified to show great variation in expertise in these dimensions. Specifically, EFL teachers self-reported inadequate knowledge of linguistics and applied linguistics. They also demonstrated insufficient knowledge of assessment in language pedagogy, lending support to the findings in Shao (2015) and Lan and Fan (2019) that EFL teachers needed training in assessment methods, self- and peer-assessment. Yet, they reported slightly higher levels of literacy in the dimension of technical skills in assessment (M=3. 83). EFL teachers also demonstrated relatively high levels of expertise in assessment principles & ethic considerations (M= 4. 0) and in awareness of students' cognitive and affective characteristics in foreign language instruction and assessment (M=4. 14).

The differential levels of competence in different dimensions are primarily related to the sources and channels through which EFL teachers acquire assessment expertise. In initial teacher education programs, pre-service EFL teachers are required to take some basic courses, such as Educational Psychology and Language Pedagogy, to lay a solid foundation for teaching. These courses cover contents related to students' cognitive and psychological characteristics to a larger or lesser degree. Data from the follow-up questionnaire showed that EFL teachers took heed of students' cognitive and affective characteristics and got to know students via different means. The most common methods were assessment (including testing, assignments, and classroom observations), communicating with students, parents, and other subject teachers, and reading related books and articles. These various factors, in combination with pre-service education, lend support to respondent EFL teachers' reported high scores on this dimension.

EFL teachers also reported relatively high scores on the dimension of assessment principles & ethic considerations. Language assessment practices and LAL are related but have different constructs. The former pertains to assessment activities, while the latter reflects how an EFL teacher perceives his or her skill level in conducting those activities. In the survey, indirect statements were developed to address this dimension for the fact that EFL teachers are not familiar with these abstract assessment terms and it does not make much sense to ask them directly how to make tests reliable or valid. This may explain why the participating EFL teachers rated themselves on the upper end of the scale even though they might not have much understanding of these abstract terms.

EFL teachers' relatively low literacy in assessment in language pedagogy could be understood from a systemic perspective. At the policy level, there are no specialized assessment policies in China. For EFL teachers, the only documents they can refer to for assessment practices is *English Curriculum Standards for Compulsory Education* (MoE, 2017) and *English Curriculum Standards for General High School* (MoE, 2022), which prescribe the bringing together of summative and formative assessment without specific guidance about assessment practices. Though formative assessment has been conducted in increasing primary and middle schools, it is considered to be "a summative mimicry of the examination system" (Xu & Brown, 2017, p. 138), because teachers' practices are reported to be heavily influenced by the long-standing testing culture in China (Q. X. Chen *et al.*, 2014). This might explain EFL teachers' reporting of relatively high scores on items addressing technical skills in assessment and assessment principles & ethic considerations.

EFL teachers' self-reported low scores on the two dimensions of knowledge of linguistics and applied linguistics and assessment in language pedagogy can be accounted for by the education experiences of these teachers with different academic degrees. Different teacher education programs have different teacher preparation courses. With regards to knowledge of linguistics and applied linguistics, a search through university programs for initial teacher education programs in Hunan and Guangdong provinces show that the vast majority of these programs offer merely the course of (Foreign) Linguistics to their four-year students, leaving the course of Applied Linguistics and other related disciplines (e. g. Second Language Acquisition, Foreign Language Teaching, Psycholinguistics) to MA teacher education programs (https://daxue. eol. cn/hun. shtml; https://daxue. eol. cn/gd. shtml). [1] Even in MA programs, only students

---

[1]   The two provinces are chosen because 97% of the respondents are from there.

who have a research orientation in foreign linguistics and applied linguistics or English education are required to take such courses. Hence, it is not difficult to understand why these EFL teachers possess inadequate knowledge of linguistics and applied linguistics. It merits our attention that in this subscale, EFL teachers scored lowest on the item relating to the CSE, which was put into practice two years before the survey. Though the CSE has become a topic of major concern in assessment research, it remains to be an unheard-of for many front-line EFL teachers. To maximize its potential in connecting teaching, learning, and assessment, administrators at different levels need to publicize the CSE so that EFL teachers could get a rich understanding of the CSE, the descriptors of language abilities at various levels, and its role in language learning.

With regards to inadequate knowledge of assessment in language pedagogy, this is mainly a result of insufficient assessment training in pre- and in-service teacher education. Despite heightened demands on teacher assessment literacy, there is only a small number of initial teacher education programs that offer mandatory or selective assessment-related courses. [1] Thus, it is critical that initial teacher education programs offer assessment-related courses to pre-service teachers.

In terms of assessment education, DeLuca and McEwen (2007) identified four different models: (1) mandatory courses targeting student assessment; (2) mandatory curriculum-based courses that integrate issues in student assessment; (3) elective courses targeting assessment and evaluation; and (4) elective curriculum-based courses with assessment concepts and practices being part of it. They found that integrating assessment within curriculum-based courses was the most common of these

---

[1]   This can be seen from the collected data that 65. 6% of the EFL teachers in the survey had received some amount of training in educational assessment/language assessment (the number is 40. 91% in the follow-up survey), whereas 34. 4% of them have no training (the number is 59. 09% in the follow-up survey).

models. Within such a context, pre-service teachers learn about assessment from instructors who typically possess no expertise in educational assessment (Quilter, 1998; Schafer, 1993), and there is little guarantee that they will receive current, appropriate, and adequate information about assessment practice, theory, and philosophy (Earl *et al.*, 2002). Even for those education programs which offer focused or embedded/integrated assessment courses, there is also a paucity of research guiding the development of effective assessment curriculum for initial teacher learning (DeLuca *et al.*, 2010). Pre-service teachers are, therefore, unlikely to acquire a comprehensive and solid understanding of assessment practice, theory, and philosophy. Hence, there is an urgent need to shift the focus of the assessment course and place more emphasis on the formative assessment.

Meanwhile, EFL teachers need to engage in professional development to become assessment literate so that they can effectively implement assessment practices to facilitate students' learning. In response to increased demands on primary and middle school teachers' professionalism, China's Ministry of Education (MoE) and Ministry of Finance (MoF) initiated the National Training Program for Primary and Middle School Teachers in 2010. The MoE promulgated *Curriculum Standards for National Training Program (Trial)* (CSNTP) in 2012, which includes different curriculum standards for teachers of different content areas, at different grade levels, and at different career stages (back-bone teachers vs. teacher educators). The CSNTP requires teacher training programs (basically short-term) at various levels to provide assessment training to in-service teachers. To standardize and facilitate the training, the MoE builds a resource library for the various courses, which include recommended resources for assessment in general education and language assessment in particular. However, in the actual delivery of these training sessions, there is no guarantee that every training program would stick to the curriculum

and offer assessment-related teaching modules as prescribed (see Dai &
Shi, 2014). Even for those programs that offer assessment training, the
focus of the course is mostly on large-scale testing and measurement. In
either case, in-service teachers might be denied the opportunity to enhance
their expertise in formative assessment.

7. 1. 3. 2   Influence of demographic characteristics on EFL teachers' LAL

A range of demographic characteristics have been researched in relation
to teacher AL/LAL, and this research focuses on the influence of such
demographics as teachers' grade levels of teaching, assessment training,
and institutional context on EFL teachers' LAL.

7. 1. 3. 2. 1   Influence of grade levels of teaching on EFL teachers' LAL

Statistical analysis of the survey results indicated that EFL teachers
from primary, junior and senior middle schools reported paralleled expertise
in the overall construct. Such a finding is consistent with previous studies
that EFL teachers (as well as teachers of different subject areas) at different
grade levels of instruction had similar classroom assessment literacy (Y. Y.
Wang, 2018; Z. C. Zhang & Burry-Stock, 2003; D. H. Zheng & Ye, 2012).

Nevertheless, teachers at different grade levels of teaching were found
to differ significantly in literacy in F5. Specifically, senior middle school
EFL teachers reported significantly higher levels of knowledge of linguistics
and applied linguistics than EFL teachers from junior and primary schools,
and junior middle school EFL teachers also reported significantly better
knowledge than primary EFL teachers. Such discrepancies in knowledge of
linguistics and applied linguistics are related to the type of education
programs the EFL teachers enrolled in, which could be inferred from the
academic degree they hold. Respondent EFL teachers in the current
research have a wide distribution in terms of academic degrees, ranging
from an associate degree to an MA degree. It is common practice in the
education system that higher levels of instruction require teachers with more

advanced academic degrees. This is in line with the fact that, in this survey, the small number of EFL teachers with an MA degree all work in senior middle schools while those with an associate degree teach in primary schools. As mentioned previously, the more advanced education programs like MA programs are more likely to offer such theory-laden courses than four-year teacher education programs. As for three-year programs, there is much less possibility for pre-service EFL teachers to take such courses. This has implications for curriculum change if we intend to prepare pre-service teachers for language assessments.

7.1.3.2.2   Influence of assessment training on EFL teachers' LAL

EFL teachers' responses to the survey revealed that significant differences existed in the overall LAL between teachers who had received some assessment training and those who hadn't, pointing to the usefulness of assessment training. In cases where there were significant differences in the dimensions, the trained EFL teachers scored significantly higher than their untrained counterparts. Data from the follow-up survey showed that 93.95% of the trained EFL teachers thought educational assessment training was fairly helpful or quite helpful. This is consistent with previous research findings that assessment training is an important factor that affects teacher AL (Alkharusi et al., 2011; DeLuca et al., 2013; Graham, 2005; Lukin et al., 2004; Mertler, 2009).

Nevertheless, the influence of assessment training is unbalanced across the five dimensions of the LAL construct. Regardless of training in assessments, EFL teachers reported similar scores on the dimensions of awareness of students' cognitive and affective characteristics and assessment principles & ethic considerations. But the EFL teachers who reported assessment training experiences demonstrated higher scores on assessment in language pedagogy, knowledge of linguistics and applied linguistics, and technical skills in assessment.

It is not unexpected that EFL teachers, trained or untrained,

demonstrate similar competence in the dimension of awareness of students'
cognitive and affective characteristics. As discussed in Subsection 7.1.3.1,
initial teacher education programs generally offer some groundwork courses
like Educational Psychology and Language Pedagogy. The inclusion of these
courses in the curricula of different education programs provides pre-service
EFL teachers with opportunities to gain a rich understanding of prospect
students' cognitive and psychological features. Furthermore, data from the
follow-up survey show EFL teachers use various means to get to understand
students' cognitive and affective characteristics.

EFL teachers also reported approximate literacy in assessment
principles & ethic considerations regardless of assessment training
experiences. This finding seems counter-intuitive, and several factors might
contribute to this. First, EFL teachers with no assessment training
experiences might lack an awareness of the complexities associated with
reliability, validity, and assessment ethics. Second, this might be related
much to the way the items addressing this dimension were designed and
phrased (indirect statements were designed to focus on EFL teachers'
assessment practices). Third, some EFL teachers seem to endorse the
assessment practices described in these items out of social desirability
(which is a major weakness of survey research), worrying that it might
threaten their faces if they choose to rate the items on the lower end of the
scale.

EFL teachers' differing competences in the dimensions of assessment in
language pedagogy and technical skills in assessment as a result of
assessment training are also expected. Items subsumed in the dimension of
assessment in language pedagogy are mainly concerned with why and how
EFL teachers conduct language assessment. Data from the follow-up survey
showed that the assessment training EFL teachers received covered the
following topics: assessment purposes (75%), assessment methods
(87.5%), writing tests (75%), describing test results (68.75%), and use

of test results (62.5%).

It is somewhat unexpected that EFL teachers who differ in assessment training experiences are also found to have differential knowledge of linguistics and applied linguistics. This might be due to the fact that some language testing and assessment textbooks (e. g. Heaton, 1998; X. J. Li, 1997) devote separate chapters to the assessment of language knowledge and skills, which enables EFL teachers to have better knowledge of linguistics and applied linguistics. Another reason might be that, in some language assessment books, introductions to language competence frameworks and models of language abilities are an important part of the content (e. g. McKay, 2006). Nevertheless, more research is needed in this area. In future studies, the type of assessment courses (educational assessment or language assessment) needs to be specified and in-depth interviews are recommended to gain a deeper understanding of the content of the assessment courses.

7. 1. 3. 2. 3   Influence of institutional context on EFL teachers' LAL

Statistics showed that responses of EFL teachers from rural, county town, and urban schools were almost indistinguishable in the overall scale and across the dimensions with the exception of F5. The finding of no significant difference in the overall LAL is consistent with previous studies that the institutional context (defined by the geographic area) is not a significant factor that might affect EFL teachers' overall competence in language assessment (Xu & Brown, 2017; D. H. Zheng & Ye, 2012; X. J. Zhao, 2014). This might be due to the fact that there is no threshold requirements of assessment competence for EFL teachers in different geographic areas. Nevertheless, county town EFL teachers were detected to report significantly higher scores than their rural counterparts on F5 (knowledge of linguistics and applied linguistics). This might be related to the threshold requirements on EFL teachers' academic degree that EFL teachers with a BA or MA degree are generally recruited in county town and urban schools. These teachers, as mentioned previously, were required to take courses of Linguistics and Applied Linguistics. Nevertheless, the varied competence in LAL areas among EFL teachers from different institutional contexts confirm the research finding of Y. Y. Wang (2018) that EFL teachers from different geographic areas might have different levels of literacy in different LAL areas. The research findings have implications for theory, policy, and practice, and could be used in the design of assessment training programs.

7.2　Implications and Applications

This section is devoted to a discussion of the implications of the research findings for theory, policy, and practice, and the applications of the findings in the design of pre- and in-service teacher education programs with a focus on the assessment component.

An LAL construct needs to incorporate both generic assessment knowledge applicable to all content areas and language specific elements to distinguish itself from general AL. It also needs to underscore situation-specific principles, values, and particularly the traditions in a specific culture (Xu & Brown, 2017), and additionally differentiate educational settings as different levels of instruction require different assessment priorities for EFL teachers.

The reported basic levels of LAL warrant the need to improve LAL of EFL teachers. AL/LAL is culturally situated and contextually sensitive, and its development and improvement is a systematic enterprise with joint efforts from appropriate stakeholders (Xu & Brown, 2016). At the macro level, policy makers need to stipulate supportive assessment policies, educational assessment standards and guidelines, and codes of ethics (Xu & Brown, 2017) to guide sound assessment practices by delineating specific principles for teachers' use of assessment to measure and support student learning within contemporary educational contexts. These professionally defined standards also need to articulate core assessment concepts and skills to provide goals for educational assessment training that constitute a stable, challenging, and long-term agenda for professional development. Assessment training grounded in such a set of professionally defined standards is potentially effective at enhancing teachers' LAL and changing their assessment practices (Ingvarson, 1998), because it offers teachers a clear understanding of what they should be getting better at doing in the classroom to improve student learning. In the meantime, teacher AL needs to be articulated as a core accomplished practice for teacher accreditation, licensure, and promotion (Gareis & Grant, 2015a; Sato et al., 2008; Xu & Brown, 2017). Additionally, a national climate in which the importance of assessment in the service of student learning needs to be set so that EFL teachers get to understand the pedagogical power of assessment and experience a need to change (Smith, 2011).

At the meso level, initial teacher education programs need to give curricular prominence to AL/LAL via discrete (language) assessment courses. The necessity of assessment education for pre-service (and in-service) teachers has been voiced by many researchers (e.g. DeLuca et al., 2010; D. L. Lin, 2016; Maclellan, 2004; Popham, 2008; Schafer, 1993; Stiggins, 2004; Vogt & Tsagari, 2014; Volante & Fazio, 2007; Xu & Brown, 2017; D. H. Zheng, 2010; D. H. Zheng & Ye, 2012). P. Chen (2005) and Maclellan (2004) consider initial teacher education programs to be a central driver for developing teachers' understandings of contemporary assessment theory and practices. Yet, there is both a paucity of research into the structure of assessment course and little agreement among teacher educators upon how assessment training is to be presented to pre-service teachers. What good assessment education looks like is subject to the interpretation of individual programs and the course instructor/teacher educator (DeLuca et al., 2010).

For assessment training to be effective, the curriculum and pedagogies need to be designed in ways that effectively facilitate pre-service EFL teachers' learning. Within a new assessment landscape which is characterized by "an accountability and standards-based orientation and a more student-directed, pedagogical stance" (DeLuca & Bellara, 2013, p. 367), there needs a strong core curriculum taught in the context of assessment practice and grounded in knowledge of students' development and learning, and an understanding of social, cultural, and educational contexts. The (language) assessment course needs not only to address key areas of assessment but also include classroom assessment as a major component to reflect teachers' practical needs, with due emphasis on various assessment methods, peer- and self-assessment, to enable pre-service EFL teachers to appreciate the complexity of language assessment and its pedagogical power as a learning tool for students. The inclusion of formative assessment as a focal point becomes a more urgent need for Chinese EFL teachers, following a dramatic decrease of tests and assignments as stipulated by the "Double Reduction" policy enacted in July, 2021. [①] Additionally, AL education needs to meet teachers' localized needs (Greenberg & Walsh, 2012; Lam, 2015; Xu & Brown, 2017). The assessment course also needs to keep a balance between language assessment theory, philosophy, and practice, and provide opportunities for pre-service EFL teachers to practice what they have learned.

Pedagogically, how to organize pre-service EFL teachers' learning experiences so that they can integrate and use their assessment knowledge in skillful ways in the classroom? This is a question of equal importance with assessment course curriculum. The teacher educator needs to advance pre-service teachers' learning of language assessment and to engage them in

---

① The General Office of the CPC Central Committee and the State Council jointly introduced a guideline in July 2021 to ease the burdens of excessive homework and off-campus tutoring for students undergoing compulsory education.

deep and complex learning about the linkages between assessment, teaching, and learning. These could be achieved through the following conditions: (1) perspective-building conversations with prospective EFL teachers to help them examine their own deep-seated beliefs and assumptions about assessments (Darling-Hammond, 2006); (2) praxis activities of connecting theory to practice (Harlen & Gardner, 2010; Russel & Loughran, 2007); (3) contextualized assessment training and modeling effective assessment practices to give pre-service EFL teachers a clear vision of language assessments (Darling-Hammond, 2006; Darling-Hammond *et al.*, 2017; Grossman, 2009), and (4) critical reflection, collaboration, and planning for learning on the part of pre-service EFL teachers (Grossman, 2009).

In terms of in-service training in assessment, sustained duration is needed and in-service EFL teachers should be provided with adequate time to learn, practice, implement, and reflect upon contemporary assessment strategies that reshape their language assessment practices. The teacher educator needs to figure out the practical needs of in-service teachers, and in the meantime, provide experiential and model-based learning experiences that enable in-service teachers to integrate and use assessment knowledge in skillful ways. S/he also needs to possess knowledge of the teachers' grade span and the school context, and provide differentiated assessment training to cater to the different needs of teachers. On one hand, EFL teachers from primary, junior and senior middle schools need different repertoires of assessment knowledge and skills to fulfill their assessment needs; on the other hand, EFL teachers from rural, county town, and urban areas might employ different strategies to assess pupils as conditioned by the school assessment policies and the resources available. To facilitate assessment training, in-service programs can take full use of online tutorials, webinars, workshops, etc. to make the training more accessible to teachers with tight schedules. In addition, school leadership needs to participate and provide support and necessary infrastructure for EFL teachers to carry out assessments.

The success of teacher assessment education is also dependent on the teacher educator. Research indicates that in some teacher education programs, teachers acquire assessment knowledge and skills from teacher educators who do not possess adequate competence in assessment (Smith, 2011), or from professionals who specialize in fields of study other than language testing and assessment (Jeong, 2013). In this case, the teacher educator needs to receive assessment training to become "experts" before teaching EFL teachers how to assess.

The ability to use a range of assessment practices to accomplish instructional goals with different students in different contexts requires highly refined knowledge and skills. Initial teacher education programs need to incorporate Linguistics and Applied Linguistics and didactic courses, in addition to assessment courses, in its curriculum to prepare pre-service EFL teachers for language assessments. These programs also need to provide opportunities for EFL teachers to get to know the CSE to enable them to get a better vision of language ability so as to better describe language learning goals. In short, EFL teachers need to incorporate subject matter goals, knowledge of language learning, and an appreciation for children's development to translate LAL into effective classroom assessment practices.

At the micro level, EFL teachers play a decisive role in developing LAL. As previous research has indicated (Deneen & Brown, 2016; Levy-Vered & Alhija, 2015; Shepard, 2006), teachers' attitudes toward and beliefs of assessment are vital in promoting AL. Hence, the first and foremost thing in developing LAL is that EFL teachers get rid of their deep-rooted belief of assessment acquired when they were students and realize the pedagogical power of assessment in facilitating student learning. Only when their CoA fits in with the current assessment requirements as conditioned by standards-based reform in education can they take the initiative to improve their competence in language assessment. With a change in CoA, EFL teachers could take full advantage of the resources available to develop their LAL through assessment training programs, professional learning community, or self-studying assessment materials.

A conclusive argument is that to promote AL/LAL of EFL teachers, there is a need to devise national assessment policies and professional assessment standards, a necessity for assessment training at different education levels, and a requirement of professional development for teacher educators. Due consideration should be given to the structure and pedagogies of assessment course to improve its efficiency in promoting teacher AL/LAL.

The research findings could be applied in the design of assessment training in initial teacher education programs and professional development programs. The initial teacher education programs could utilize the LAL model as a reference and offer courses of Linguistics and Applied Linguistics, in addition to educational/language assessment courses, to equip pre-service EFL teachers with adequate assessment knowledge. For assessment courses to be effective, textbook writers need to incorporate those content areas that are most relevant to EFL teachers' classroom assessment practices and reflective of the current assessment landscape. The professional development programs could use the empirically reduced questionnaire to diagnose in-service EFL teachers' strengths and weaknesses in LAL, and design assessment content accordingly to make the training more effective.

7.3 Summary

This chapter reviews the three research questions and discusses the results. The proposed LAL model is indicative of assessment policy initiatives in China and the contemporary assessment landscape in the globe by incorporating assessment for learning in its components. Its preliminary validity is established through feedback from experienced EFL teachers and experts in the assessment community, and further supported by the data from the large-scale survey.

The construction of the LAL measuring instrument is a complex, iterative process. Due attention is paid to the limitations inherent in the questionnaire. Data from the follow-up survey also confirm some of the results about EFL teachers' levels of LAL. The research findings have implications for theory, policy, and practice. The successful improvement of EFL teachers' LAL is contingent on a plethora of factors at national, aggregate, and individual levels. It becomes a joint enterprise requiring support from different stakeholder groups, such as policy makers, school administrators, teacher educators, students, and even the general public. Still, EFL teachers remain to be the main drivers of their LAL development. They need to make full use of classroom assessment practices to gain a better understanding of assessment processes, engage in conversations and collaboration with colleagues, and participate in assessment training provided by professional development programs.

CHAPTER EIGHT
CONCLUSION

8.1   Major Findings of the Research

The research reported in this book aims to examine the LAL of Chinese EFL teachers. With a synthesis of research literature on AL and LAL, major professional standards for teachers, and prominent assessment standards documents, the LAL for Chinese EFL teachers was unpacked as comprising five dimensions, i. e. knowledge of assessment in language pedagogy, knowledge of linguistics and applied linguistics, awareness of students' cognitive and affective characteristics, technical skills in assessment, and assessment principles & ethic considerations.

A questionnaire was developed to measure EFL teachers' current LAL levels. The validity of the instrument was established through expert judgement and piloting. Then a large-scale survey was launched online to collect EFL teachers' responses. EFA of the data indicated satisfactory psychometric property of the measuring tool and suggested a five-factor structure of LAL, which was in line with the components hypothesized in this research. The final version of the LAL instrument included 40 items and could be used in future research.

The survey results indicated that EFL teachers had a basic level of competence in language assessment and they needed professional development to become effective in assessment practices. In terms of the influence of demographic characteristics on LAL levels, assessment training was found to have significant effect on EFL teachers' overall competence and literacy levels in knowledge of assessment in language pedagogy, knowledge of linguistics and applied linguistics, technical skills in assessment, and assessment principles & ethic considerations. The other two demographic characteristics investigated in this research, i. e. grade levels of teaching and institutional context, were found not to be significantly related to the EFL teachers' overall LAL and literacy levels in the dimensions except for knowledge of linguistics and applied linguistics.

8.2   Contributions of the Research

Research on teachers' LAL is a vibrant field of enquiry in the globe. This field has yielded a body of knowledge that conceptualizes LAL in a variety of ways. The current study does not intend to find "the" one definition of LAL and construct the assessment-of-LAL measuring instrument. Rather, it intends to clarify the construct and its measurement in a specific educational context by sketching conceptual controversies and assessment approaches. This piece of research makes several contributions to the existent literature.

First, this study addresses a research gap by conceptualizing LAL in the Chinese educational context and developing a model of LAL for primary and middle school EFL teachers. The development of the theoretical model was built on an extensive analysis of standards documents (professional standards for teachers and prominent assessment standards) and a thorough understanding of the latest developments in AL and LAL theories. With close attention to China's EFL educational context, this model highlights the importance of awareness of students' cognitive and affective characteristics in foreign language teaching and assessment.

Second, a reliable and valid LAL measuring instrument was constructed based on the proposed LAL model. The items in the instrument were drawn upon standards documents and existing literature in assessment, linguistics, pedagogy, educational psychology, etc. to ensure that the items constructed were age-related, situation-sensitive, culturally appropriate, and subject-specific. As AL/LAL might vary with curriculum standards, educational settings, and socio-political contexts, this local research would be helpful for generating essential components for LAL driven by practical needs (e. g. Vogt & Tsagari, 2014; Xu & Brown, 2017). This instrument might be used to identify the needs of in-service EFL teachers and to develop appropriate training programs. It might also have implications for pre-service EFL teacher education programs in preparing future teachers for language assessment practices.

Third, statistical analyses were conducted to investigate whether differences existed in LAL levels among EFL teachers working at different levels of instruction. To our best knowledge, this is one of the first empirical studies of the same kind in China. The research finding that EFL teachers of different grade levels of teaching differed significantly in terms of knowledge of linguistics and applied linguistics has implications for curriculum reform for teacher education programs.

8.3 Limitations and Suggestions for Further Research

The complex notion of LAL is conceptualized as "complex ability constructs that are context-specific, trainable, and closely related to real life" (Koeppen et al., 2008, p. 61). The defining and measuring of such a complex construct are a time-consuming and resource-intensive undertaking and present great challenges to researchers. Due to the author's limited sources, inadequate time and energy, there are admittedly inadequacies in the LAL conceptualization and elements of LAL that are not adequately captured in the measuring instrument. Suggestions for future studies include: (1) triangulating the quantitative data with interviews, think-aloud protocols, and other qualitative methods to establish how items are understood; (2) cooperating with representatives of other disciplines (e. g. educational psychology researchers and domain experts) and incorporating the perspectives of different stakeholders (especially the practising teachers) in establishing a model of LAL; and (3) more empirical research for construct validation of the instrument with the use of more powerful statistical analysis (i. e. confirmatory factor analysis).

Another limitation of the current research lies in the generalizability of the research findings of EFL teachers' self-perceived LAL levels by its use of a self-reported questionnaire survey and a non-random sampling technique. Although an online questionnaire is accessible to a large sample, it is possible that participants overestimate on questionnaire items based on their own understandings (G. T. L. Brown, 2004) or out of social desirability reasons (Dörnyei & Taguchi, 2010). As a consequence, responses may reflect what EFL teachers think they should be/do, rather than what they actually are/do or be able to do. In addition, interpretation of responses may rely too heavily on quantitative analysis. Validity considerations call for investigating EFL teachers' real-life classroom assessment practices. As a consequence, the research findings need to be considered in light of these limitations and are not extended to EFL teachers in the whole nation.

Though achieving sufficient reliability and generalizability in LAL assessments is challenging given the complex nature of the construct, further research is recommended with a triangulation of data through depth interviews, classroom observations, and other data gathering to deepen our understanding of EFL teachers' LAL levels. Moreover, for future research, the questionnaire survey could be sent to a more representative sample across the country.

A further limitation was investigating EFL teachers' LAL in isolation from their CoA. There might be a discrepancy (even a conflict) between the two. As a consequence, it is highly recommended that further research takes into account EFL teachers' CoA to arrive at a better understanding of the relationship between beliefs and LAL.

References

ADIE L, 2013. The development of teacher assessment identity through participation in online moderation[J]. Assessment in education: principles, policy & practice, 20(1): 91-106.

AERA, APA, NCME, 2014. Standards for educational and psychological testing [M]. Washington, D. C. : American Educational Research Association.

AFT, NCME, NEA, 1990. Standards for teacher competence in educational assessment of students[S/OL]. Washington, D. C.: National Council on Measurement in Education[2019-12-10]. https://buros. org/standards-teacher-competence-educational-assessment-students.

AIRASIAN P W, RUSSELL M, 2007. Classroom assessment: concepts and applications(5th ed.)[M]. Blacklick, OH: McGraw-Hill.

ALDERSON J C, 2005. Diagnosing foreign language proficiency: the interface between learning and assessment[M]. London: Continuum.

ALKHARUSI H, KAZEM A M, AL-MUSAWAI A, 2011. Knowledge, skills, and attitudes of preservice and inservice teachers in educational measurement[J]. Asia-Pacific journal of teacher education, 39 (2): 113-123.

ALLAL L, 2013. Teachers' professional judgement in assessment: a cognitive act and a socially situated practice[J]. Assessment in education: principles, policy & practice, 20(1): 20-34.

ANDRADE H L, 2013. Classroom assessment in the context of

learning theory and research[M]//McMillan J H. SAGE handbook of research on classroom assessment. Thousand Oaks: SAGE: 17-34.

ANDRADE H L, HERITAGE M, 2018. Using formative assessment to enhance learning, achievement, and academic self-regulation[M]. New York: Routledge.

ARKSEY H, ALLEYWAY L, 2005. Scoping studies: towards a methodological framework[J]. International journal of social research methodology, 8(1): 19-32.

BACHMAN L F, COHEN A D, 1998. Interfaces between second language acquisition and language testing research[M]. Cambridge: Cambridge University Press.

BACHMAN L F, PALMER A S, 2010. Language assessment in practice: developing language assessments and justifying their use in the real world[M]. Oxford: Oxford University Press.

BAKER B A, RICHES C, 2018. The development of EFL examinations in Haiti: collaboration and language assessment literacy development[J]. Language testing, 35(4): 557-581.

BARNES N, FIVES H, DACEY C D, 2017. US teachers' conceptions of the purposes of assessment[J]. Teaching and teacher education, 65: 107-116.

BLACK P, WILIAM D, 1998. Assessment and classroom learning [J]. Assessment in education: principles, policy & practice, 5(1): 7-74.

BOL L, STRAGE A, 1996. The contradiction between teachers' instructional goals and their assessment practices in high school biology courses[J]. Science education, 80(2): 145-163.

BORAIE D, 2015. The construct of language assessment literacy as perceived by foreign language teachers in a specific context[C]. Paper presented at the 37th Language Testing and Research Colloquium, Toronto, Canada, March 18-20.

BORG S, 2003. Teacher cognition in language teaching: a review of research on what language teachers think, know, believe, and do[J]. Language teaching, 36(2): 81-109.

BORKO H, MAYFIELD V, MARION S, et al. 1997. Teacher's professional knowledge landscapes: teacher stories—stories of teachers—school stories—stories of schools[J]. Educational researcher, 25(3): 24-30.

BREEN M P, BARRATT-PUGH C, DEREWIANKA B, et al. 1997. Profiling ESL children: how teachers interpret and use national and state assessment frameworks (Vol. 1): key issues & findings[R]. Canberra, Australia. Commonwealth Department of Employment, Education, Training and Youth Affairs.

BRIGHT G W, JOYNER J M, 1998. Understanding and improving classroom assessment: summary of issues raised[C]//Bright G W, Joyner J M. Classroom assessment in mathematics: views from a National Science Foundation Working Conference (Greensboro, North Carolina, May 16-18, 1997). Lanham, MD: University Press of America, Inc.: 27-57.

BRINDLEY G, 2001. Language assessment and professional development[M]// Elder C, Brown A, Grove E, et al. Experimenting with uncertainty: essays in honour of Alan Davies. Cambridge: Cambridge University Press: 126-136.

BROADFOOT P M, 1996. Educational assessment: the myth of measurement [M]//Woods P. Contemporary issues in teaching and learning. London: Routledge: 203-230.

BROADFOOT P M, 2005. Dark alleys and blind bends: testing the language of learning[J]. Language testing, 22(2): 123-141.

BROOKHART S M, 2001. The "standards" and classroom assessment research[C]. Paper presented at the Annual Meeting of the American Association of Colleges for Teacher Education, 53rd, Dallas, TX, March 1-4.

BROOKHART S M, 2011. Educational assessment knowledge and

skills for teachers[J]. Educational measurement: issues and practice, 30 (1): 3-12.

BROWN G T L, 2004. Teachers' conceptions of assessment: implications for policy and professional development[J]. Assessment in education: principles, policy & practice, 11(3): 301-318.

BROWN G T L, 2006. Teachers' conceptions of assessment: validation of an abridged version[J]. Psychological reports, 99(1): 166-170.

BROWN G T L, 2008. Conceptions of assessment: understanding what assessment means to teachers and students[M]. New York: Nova Science Publishers.

BROWN G T L, 2011a. Self-regulation of assessment beliefs and attitudes: a review of the students' conceptions of assessment inventory[J]. Educational psychology, 31(6): 731-748.

BROWN G T L, 2011b. Teachers' conceptions of assessment: comparing primary and secondary teachers in New Zealand[J]. Assessment matters, 3: 45-70.

BROWN G T L, HUI S K F, FLORA W M, et al. 2011. Teachers' conceptions of assessment in Chinese contexts: a tripartite model of accountability, improvement, and irrelevance[J]. International journal of educational research, 50(5-6): 307-320.

BROWN G T L, REMESAL A, 2012. Prospective teachers' conceptions of assessment: a cross-cultural comparison[J]. The Spanish journal of psychology, 15(1): 75-89.

BROWN G T L, GAO L B, 2015. Chinese teachers' conceptions of assessment for and of learning: six competing and complementary purposes [J]. Cogent education, 2: 993836.

BROWN G T L, HARRIS L R, 2009. Unintended consequences of using tests to improve learning: how improvement-oriented resources heighten conceptions of assessment as school accountability[J]. Journal of multi-disciplinary evaluation, 6(12): 68-91.

BROWN J D, BAILEY K M, 2008. Language testing courses: what are they in 2007? [J]. Language testing, 25(3): 349-383.

BUCK G A, TRAUTH-NARE A E, 2009. Preparing teachers to make the formative assessment process integral to science teaching and learning [J]. Journal of science teacher education, 20(5): 475-494.

BUTLER Y G, 2018. The role of context in young learners' processes for responding to self-assessment items[J]. The modern language journal, 102(1): 242-261.

BUTLER Y G, 2019. Assessment of young English learners in instructional settings[M]//Gao A. Second handbook of English language teaching. Cham: Springer: 477-495.

BUTLER Y G, LEE J Y, 2010. The effects of self-assessment among young learners of English[J]. Language testing, 27(1): 5-31.

BUTLER Y G, PENG X L, LEE J Y, 2021. Young learners' voices: towards a learner-centered approach to understanding language assessment literacy[J]. Language testing, 38(3): 429-455.

BUYUKKARCI K, 2014. Assessment beliefs and practices of language teachers in primary education[J]. International journal of instruction, 7 (1): 107-120.

BYRNES H, 2006. What kind of resource is language and why does it matter for advanced language learning[M]//Byrnes H. Advanced language learning: the contribution of Halliday and Vygotsky. London: Continuum: 1-28.

CAMPBELL C, MURPHY J A, HOLT J K, 2002. Psychometric analysis of an assessment literacy instrument: applicability to pre-service teachers[C]. Paper presented at the Annual Meeting of the Mid-western Educational Research Association. Columbus, OH.

CAMPBELL C, EVANS J A, 2000. Investigation of pre-service teachers' classroom assessment practices during student teaching[J]. The journal of educational research, 93(6): 350-355.

CARLESS D, LAM R, 2014. The examined life: perspectives of lower primary school students in Hong Kong[J]. Education, 42(3): 313-329.

CCSSO, 2011. Interstate teacher assessment and support consortium (InTASC) model core teaching standards: a resource for state dialogue[R]. Washington, D. C.: the Council of Chief State School Officers.

CHAPPUIS S J, 2015. Seven strategies of assessment for learning [M]. New York: Pearson.

CHAPPUIS S J, CHAPPUIS J, STIGGINS R J, 2009. Supporting teacher learning teams[J]. Educational leadership, 66(5): 56-60.

CHEN P, 2005. Teacher candidates' assessment literacy[J]. Academic exchange quarterly, 62(5): 62-66.

CHEN Q X, MAY L, KLENOWSKI V, et al. 2014. The enactment of formative assessment in English language classrooms in two Chinese universities: teacher and student responses[J]. Assessment in education: principles, policy & practice, 21(3): 271-285.

CHENG L Y, DELUCA C, 2011. Voices from test-takers: further evidence for language assessment validation and use [J]. Educational assessment, 16(2): 104-122.

CHENG L Y, ROGERS W T, WANG X Y, 2008. Assessment purposes and procedures in ESL/EFL classrooms [J]. Assessment & evaluation in higher education, 33(1): 9-32.

CHILD D, 2006. The essentials of factor analysis (3rd ed.)[M]. New York: Continuum.

CLARK L A, WATSON D, 1995. Constructing validity: basic issues in objective scale development[J]. Psychological assessment, 7(3): 309-319.

CLARKE S, GIPPS C, 2000. The role of teachers in teacher assessment in England 1996—1998[J]. Evaluation & research in education, 14(1): 38-52.

COLBY-KELLY C, TURNER C E, 2007. AFL research in the L2 classroom and evidence of usefulness: taking formative assessment to the next level[J]. Canadian modern language review, 64(1): 9-37.

COLLINS S, REISS M, STOBART G, 2010. What happens when high-stakes testing stops? Teachers' perceptions of the impact of compulsory national testing in science of 11-year-olds in England and its abolition in Wales[J]. Assessment in education: principles, policy & practice, 17(3): 273-286.

COMREY A L, LEE H B, 1992. A first course in factor analysis (2nd ed.)[M]. Hillsdale, NJ: Lawrence Eribaum Associates.

CONNOLLY S, KLENOWSKI V, WYATT-SMITH C M, 2012. Moderation and consistency of teacher judgement: teachers' views[J]. British educational research journal, 38(4): 593-614.

COOKSEY R W, FREEBODY P, WYATT-SMITH C, 2007. Assessment as judgment-in-context: analyzing how teachers evaluate students' writing[J]. Educational research and evaluation, 13(5): 401-434.

COWIE B, CARR M, 2004. The consequences of socio-cultural assessment[M]// Cowie B, Carr M. Early childhood education: society and culture. London: SAGE: 95-106.

CRUSAN D, PLAKANS L, GEBRIL A, 2016. Writing assessment literacy: surveying second language teachers' knowledge, beliefs, and practices[J]. Assessing writing, 28: 43-56.

CSIZÉR K, DÖRNYEI Z, 2005. Language learners' motivational profiles and their motivated learning behavior[J]. Language learning, 55(4): 613-659.

CUMMING J J, MAXWELL G S, 2004. Assessment in Australian schools: current practice and trends[J]. Assessment in education, 11(1): 89-108.

CUMMINS J J, 1979. Linguistic interdependence and the educational development of bilingual children[J]. Review of educational research, 49

(2): 222-251.

CZERNIAK C M, LUMPE A T, 1996. Relationship between teacher beliefs and science education reform [J]. Journal of science teacher education, 7(4): 247-266.

DANIELSON C, 2013. The framework for teaching evaluation instrument (2nd ed.)[M]. Princeton, NJ: Danielson Group.

DANILI E, REID N, 2006. Cognitive factors that can potentially affect pupils' test performance [J]. Chemistry education research and practice, 7(2): 64-83.

DARLING-HAMMOND L, 2006. Constructing 21st-century teacher education[J]. Journal of teacher education, 57(3): 300-314.

DARLING-HAMMOND L, HYLER M E, GARDNER M, 2017. Effective teacher professional development[M]. Palo Alto, CA: Learning Policy Institute.

DAVIES A, 1990. Principles of language testing [M]. Oxford: Blackwell.

DAVIES A, 2008. Textbook trends in teaching language testing[J]. Language testing, 25(3): 327-347.

DAVISON C, 2004. The contradictory culture of teacher-based assessment: ESL teacher assessment practices in Australian and Hong Kong secondary schools[J]. Language testing, 21(3): 305-334.

DAVISON C, LEUNG C, 2009. Current issues in English language teacher-based assessment[J]. TESOL quarterly, 43(3): 393-415.

DELUCA C, MCEWEN L, 2007. Evaluating assessment curriculum in teacher education programs: an evaluation process paper [C]. Paper presented at the Annual Edward F. Kelly Evaluation Conference, Ottawa, ON, April.

DELUCA C, KLINGER D A, 2010. Assessment literacy development: identifying gaps in teacher candidates' learning [J]. Assessment in education: principles, policy & practice, 17(4): 419-438.

DELUCA C, CHAVEZ T, BELLARA A, et al. 2013. Pedagogies for preservice assessment education: supporting teacher candidates' assessment literacy development[J]. The teacher educator, 48(2): 128-142.

DELUCA C, COOMBS A J, MACGREGOR S, et al. 2019a. Toward a differential and situated view of assessment literacy: studying teachers' responses to classroom assessment scenarios[J]. Frontiers in education, 4: 1-10.

DELUCA C, COOMBS A J, LAPOINTE-MCEWAN D, 2019b. Assessment mindset: exploring the relationship between teacher mindset and approaches to classroom assessment[J]. Studies in educational evaluation, 61: 159-169.

DELUCA C, KLINGER D A, SEARLE M, et al. 2010. Developing a curriculum for assessment education[J]. Assessment matters, 2: 20-42.

DELUCA C, LAPOINTE-MCEWAN D, LUHANGA U, 2016a. Approaches to classroom assessment inventory: a new instrument to support teacher assessment literacy[J]. Educational assessment, 21(4): 248-266.

DELUCA C, LAPOINTE-MCEWAN D, LUHANGA U, 2016b. Teacher assessment literacy: a review of international standards and measures[J]. Educational assessment, evaluation and accountability, 28 (3): 251-272.

DENEEN C, BOUD D, 2014. Patterns of resistance in managing assessment change[J]. Assessment & evaluation in higher education, 39 (5): 577-591.

DENEEN C, BROWN G T L, 2011. The persistence of vision: an analysis of continuity and change in conceptions of assessment within a teacher education program [C]. Paper presented at the 37th Annual Conference of the International Association of Educational Assessment (IAEA) on "Assessment and the Challenge of Globalization". Manila, Philippines, Nov. 23-28.

DENEEN C, BROWN G T L, 2016. The impact of conceptions of assessment on assessment literacy in a teacher education program[J]. Cogent education, 3(1): 1225380.

DÖRNYEI Z, 1998. Motivation in second and foreign language learning[J]. Language teaching, 31(3): 117-135.

DÖRNYEI Z, 2003. Attitudes, orientations, and motivations in language learning: advances in theory, research, and applications[J]. Language learning, 53(S1): 3-32.

DÖRNYEI Z, TAGUCHI T, 2010. Questionnaires in second language research: construction, administration, and processing (2nd ed.) [M]. New York: Routledge.

DUBOC A P M, 2009. Language assessment from the perspective of the new literacy studies[J]. Lenguaje, 36 (2): 159-178.

EARL L, FREEMAN S, LASKY S, et al. 2002. Policy, politics, pedagogy and people: early perceptions and challenges of large-scale reform in Ontario secondary schools[R]. International Centre for Educational Change, the Ontario Institute for Studies in Education of the University of Toronto.

ELLIS R, 1994. Factors in the incidental acquisition of second language vocabulary from oral input: a review essay[J]. Applied language learning, 5(1): 1-32.

ENGELSEN K S, SMITH K, 2014. Assessment literacy[M]//Wyatt-Smith C, Klenowski V, Colbert P. Designing assessment for quality learning. Dordrecht: Springer: 91-107.

FALSGRAF C, 2006. Why a national assessment summit? [C]// Rosenbusch M H. New Visions in Action: National Assessment Summit Papers. Ames, IA: Iowa State University: 5-8.

FENWICK L, 2017. Promoting assessment for learning through curriculum-based performance standards: teacher responses in the Northern Territory of Australia[J]. The curriculum journal, 28(1): 41-58.

FLEER M, 2015. Developing an assessment pedagogy: the tensions and struggles in re-theorising assessment from a cultural-historical perspective[J]. Assessment in education: principles, policy & practice, 22 (2): 224-246.

FLÓREZ PETOUR T, 2014. Systems, ideologies and history: a three-dimensional absence in the study of assessment reform processes [J]. Assessment in education: principles, policy & practice, 22(1): 3-26.

FORSBERG E, WERMKE W, 2012. Knowledge sources and autonomy: German and Swedish teachers' continuing professional development of assessment knowledge [J]. Professional development in education, 38(5): 741-758.

FREY N, FISHER D, 2009. Using common formative assessments as a source of professional development in an urban American elementary school[J]. Teaching and teacher education, 25(5): 674-680.

FULCHER G, 2012. Assessment literacy for the language classroom [J]. Language assessment quarterly, 9(2): 113-132.

FULMER G W, LEE I C H, TAN K H K, 2015. Multi-level model of contextual factors and teachers' assessment practices: an integrative review of research[J]. Assessment in education: principles, policy & practice, 22 (4): 475-494.

GARDNER R C, 2001. Integrative motivation and second language acquisition[J]. Motivation and second language acquisition, 23(1): 1-19.

GARDNER R C, LAMBERT W E, 1972. Attitudes and motivation in second language learning[M]. Rowley, Mass: Newbury House Publishers, Inc.

GAREIS C R, GRANT L W, 2015a. Assessment literacy for teacher candidates: a focused approach[J]. Teacher educators' journal, 2: 4-21.

GAREIS C R, GRANT L W, 2015b. Teacher-made assessments: how to connect curriculum, instruction, and student learning (2nd ed.) [M]. New York: Routledge.

GIRALDO F, 2018. Language assessment literacy: implications for language teachers[M]. Profile issues in teachers' professional development, 20(1): 179-195.

GOLDSTEIN I L, 1991. Training in work organizations [M]// Dunnette M D, Hough L M. Handbook of industrial and organizational psychology (Vol. 3). Palo Alto: Consulting Psychologists Press: 507-619.

GOTCH C, FRENCH B, 2014. A systematic review of assessment literacy measures [J]. Educational measurement: issues and practice, 33 (2): 14-18.

GOTTHEINER D M, SIEGEL M A, 2012. Experienced middle school science teachers' assessment literacy: investigating knowledge of students' conceptions in genetics and ways to shape instruction[J]. Journal of science teacher education, 23(5): 531-557.

GRAHAM P, 2005. Classroom-based assessment: changing knowledge and practice through pre-service teacher education[J]. Teaching and teacher education, 21(6): 607-621.

GREENBERG J, WALSH K, 2012. What teacher preparation programs teach about K-12 Assessment: a review[R]. National Council on Teacher Quality.

GROSSMAN P, 2009. Research on pedagogical approaches in teacher education [M]//Cochran-Smith M, Zeichner K M. Studying teacher education: the report of the AERA panel on research and teacher education. New York: Routledge: 437-488.

GU P Y Q, 2014. The unbearable lightness of the curriculum: what drives the assessment practices of a teacher of English as a foreign language in a Chinese secondary school? [J]. Assessment in education: principles, policy & practice, 21(3): 286-305.

GULLICKSON A R, 1993. Matching measurement instruction to classroom-based evaluation: perceived discrepancies, needs, and challenges [M]//Wise S. Teacher training in measurement and assessment skills.

Lincoln, NE: University of Nebraska-Lincoln: 1-25.

GUNN A C, GILMORE A, 2014. Early childhood initial teacher education students' learning about assessment[J]. Assessment matters, 7 (2): 24-38.

HAMP-LYONS L, 2017. Language assessment literacy for learning-oriented language assessment [J]. Papers in language testing and assessment, 6(1): 88-111.

HARDING L, BRUNFAUT T, 2020. Trajectories of language assessment literacy in a teacher-researcher partnership: locating elements of praxis through narrative inquiry[M]//Poehner M, Inbar-Lourie O. Toward a reconceptualization of second language classroom assessment. New York: Springer: 61-81.

HARDING L, KREMMEL B, 2016. Teacher assessment literacy and professional development[M]//Tsagari D, Banerjee J. Handbook of second language assessment. Boston: De Gruyter Mouton: 413-428.

HARLEN W, GARDNER J, 2010. Assessment to support learning [M]//Gardner J, Harlen W, Hayward L, et al. Developing teacher assessment. New York: Open University Press: 15-28.

HARRIS L R, BROWN G T L, 2009. The complexity of teachers' conceptions of assessment: tensions between the needs of schools and students[J]. Assessment in education: principles, policy & practice, 16 (3): 365-381.

HARRISON C, 2005. Teachers developing assessment for learning: mapping teacher change[J]. Teacher development, 9(2): 255-263.

HASSELGREEN A, CARLSEN C, HELNESS H, 2004. European survey of language testing and assessment needs: general findings (needs assessment No. 1)[R]. Bergen: University of Bergen.

HATTIE J, 2009. The black box of tertiary assessment: an impending revolution[M]//Meyer L H, Davidson S, Anderson H, et al. Tertiary assessment & higher education student outcomes: policy, practice &

research. Wellington, New Zealand: Ako Aotearoa: 259-275.

HEATON J B, 1988. Writing English language tests (2nd ed.) [M]. London: Longman.

HERPPICH S, PRAETORIUS A K, FÖRSTER N, et al. 2018. Teachers' assessment competence: Integrating knowledge-, process-, and product-oriented approaches into a competence-oriented conceptual model [J]. Teaching and teacher education, 76: 181-193.

HIDRI S, 2021. Perspectives on language assessment literacy—challenges for improved student learning[M]. New York: Routledge.

HOOVER N R, 2009. A descriptive study of teachers' instructional use of student assessment data[D]. Virginia Commonwealth University, Richmond, VA.

HUHTA A, HIRVALÄ T, BANERJEE J, 2005. European survey of language testing and assessment needs (part 2): regional findings[R]. Gothenburg, Sweden: European Association for Language Testing and Assessment [2020-12-12]. http://users. jyu. fi/~huhta/ENLTA2/First_page. html.

INBAR-LOURIE O. 2008a. Constructing a language assessment knowledge base: a focus on language assessment courses[J]. Language testing, 25(3): 385-402.

INBAR-LOURIE O, 2008b. Language assessment culture [M]// Shohamy E, Hornberger N. Encyclopedia of language and education (Vol. 7). New York: Springer: 285-300.

INBAR-LOURIE O, 2013. Language assessment literacy: what are the ingredients[C]. Paper presented at the 4th CBLA SIG Symposium Programme, University of Cyprus, Nov. 1-2.

INBAR-LOURIE, O, 2017. Language assessment literacies and the language testing community: a mid-life identity crisis[C]. Paper presented at the Language Testing Research Colloquium, Bogotá, Colombia, July 17-21.

INGVARSON L, 1998. Professional development as the pursuit of professional standards: the standards-based professional development system[J]. Teaching and teacher education, 14(1): 127-140.

JEONG H, 2013. Defining assessment literacy: is it different for language testers and non-language testers? [J]. Language testing, 30(3): 345-362.

JIN Y, 2010. The place of language testing and assessment in the professional preparation of foreign language teachers in China[J]. Language testing, 27(4): 555-584.

JONES A, MORELAND J, 2005. The importance of pedagogical content knowledge in assessment for learning practices: a case-study of a whole-school approach[J]. Curriculum journal, 16(2): 193-206.

KAHL S R, HOFMAN P, BRYANT S, 2013. Assessment literacy standards and performance measures for teacher candidates and practicing teachers[R]. Paper prepared for the Council for the Accreditation of Educator Preparation (CAEP). Dover, NH: Measured Progress.

KAISER J, SÜDKAMP A, MÖLLER J, 2017. The effects of student characteristics on teachers' judgment accuracy: disentangling ethnicity, minority status, and achievement[J]. Journal of educational psychology, 109(6): 871-888.

KARAGUL B I, YUKSEL D, ALTAY M, 2017. Assessment and grading practices of EFL teachers in Turkey[J]. International journal of language academy, 5(5): 168-174.

KING J D, 2010. Criterion-referenced assessment literacy of educators [D]. Hattiesburg: University of Southern Mississippi.

KLEINSASSER R C, 2005. Transforming a postgraduate level assessment course: a second language teacher educator's narrative[J]. Prospect, 20(3): 77-102.

KOEPPEN K, HARTIG J, KLIEME E, et al. 2008. Current issues in competence modeling and assessment [J]. Zeitschrift für psychologie/

Journal of psychology, 216(2): 61-73.

KOH K H, 2011. Improving teachers' assessment literacy through professional development[J]. Teaching education, 22(3): 255-276.

KOLOI-KEAIKITSE S, 2012. Classroom assessment practices: a survey of Botswana primary and secondary school teachers[D]. Muncie: Ball State University.

KREMMEL B, HARDING L, 2020. Towards a comprehensive, empirical model of language assessment literacy across stakeholder groups: developing the language assessment literacy survey[J]. Language assessment quarterly, 17(1): 100-120.

KUNNAN A J, 2004. Test fairness[C]//Milanovic M, Weir C J. Europe language testing in a global context: proceedings of the ALTE Barcelona Conference. Cambridge: Cambridge University Press: 27-48.

KVASOVA O, KAVYTSKA T, 2014. The assessment competence of university foreign language teachers: a Ukrainian perspective[J]. Language learning in higher education, 4(1): 159-177.

LAM R, 2015. Language assessment training in Hong Kong: implications for language assessment literacy[J]. Language testing, 32(2): 169-197.

LAM R, 2019. Teacher assessment literacy: surveying knowledge, conceptions and practices of classroom-based writing assessment in Hong Kong[J]. System, 81: 78-89.

LAMBERT C, PHILP J, NAKAMURA S, 2017. Learner-generated content and engagement in second language task performance[J]. Language teaching research, 21(6): 665-680.

LAN C S, FAN S Y, 2019. Developing classroom-based language assessment literacy for in-service EFL teachers: the gaps[J]. Studies in educational evaluation, 61: 112-122.

LEE C, WILIAM D, 2005. Studying changes in the practice of two teachers developing assessment for learning[J]. Teacher development, 9

(2): 265-283.

LEE J Y, 2019. A training project to develop teachers' assessment literacy[M]//White E, Delaney T. Handbook of research on assessment literacy and teacher-made testing in the language classroom. Hershey: IGI Global: 58-80.

LEIGHTON J P, GOKIERT R J, COR M K, et al. 2010. Teacher beliefs about the cognitive diagnostic information of classroom-versus large-scale tests: implications for assessment literacy [J]. Assessment in education: principles, policy & practice, 17(1): 7-21.

LEONG W S, 2014. Knowing the intentions, meaning and context of classroom assessment: a case study of Singaporean teacher's conception and practice[J]. Studies in educational evaluation, 43: 70-78.

LEUNG C, 2004. Developing formative teacher assessment: knowledge, practice, and change[J]. Language assessment quarterly, 1 (1): 19-41.

LEUNG C, 2014. Classroom-based assessment issues for language teacher education [M]//Kunnan A. Evaluation, methodology, and interdisciplinary themes (Vol. 3). Chichester, UK: Wiley Blackwell: 1510-1519.

LEVY-VERED A, ALHIJA F N, 2015. Modelling beginning teachers' assessment literacy: the contribution of training, self-efficacy, and conceptions of assessment[J]. Educational research and evaluation, 21(5-6): 378-406.

LIN L, LI G Y, GUO X J, 2021. Pre-service Chinese language teachers' conceptions of assessment: a person-centered perspective[J]. Language teaching research, 0(0): 1-23.

LOEWEN S, GONULAL T, 2015. Exploratory factor analysis and principal components analysis [M]//Plonsky L. Advancing quantitative methods in second language research. New York: Routledge: 182-212.

LOONEY A, CUMMING J, VAN DER KLEIJ F, et al. 2017.

Conceptualizing the role of teachers as assessors: teacher assessment identity[J]. Assessment in education: principles, policy & practice, 25 (5): 442-467.

LOPEZ L M, PASQUINI R, 2017. Professional controversies between teachers about their summative assessment practices: a tool for building assessment capacity[J]. Assessment in education: principles, policy & practice, 24(2): 228-249.

LOUGHRAN J, 2007. Enacting a pedagogy of teacher education [M]//RUSSEL T, LOUGHRAN J. Enacting a pedagogy of teacher education: values, relationships and practices. London: Routledge: 11-25.

LUKIN L E, BANDALOS D L, ECKHOUT T J, et al. 2004. Facilitating the development of assessment literacy [J]. Educational measurement: issues and practice, 23(2): 26-32.

MACLELLAN E, 2004. Initial knowledge states about assessment: novice teachers' conceptualizations[J]. Teaching and teacher education, 20 (5): 523-535.

MARZANO R J, 2013. Art and science of teaching/asking questions— at four different levels[J]. Educational leadership, 70(5): 76-77.

MCKAY P, 2006. Assessing young language learners[M]. Oxford: Oxford University Press.

MCMILLAN J H, 2000. Fundamental assessment principles for teachers and school administrators[J]. Practical assessment, research, and evaluation, 7: Article 8. DOI: https://doi.org/10.7275/5kc4-jy05.

MCMORRIS R F, BOOTHROYD R A, 1993. Tests that teachers build: an analysis of classroom tests in science and mathematics [J]. Applied measurement in education, 6(4): 321-342.

MCNAMARA T, ROEVER C, 2006. Psychometric approaches to fairness: bias and DIF[J]. Language learning, 56(Suppl 2): 81-128.

MEDE E, ATAY D, 2017. English language teachers' assessment literacy: the Turkish context[J]. Dil dergisi, 1: 43-60.

MERTLER C A, 2003. Pre-service versus in-service teachers' assessment literacy: does classroom experience make a difference? [C]. Paper presented at the Annual Meeting of the Mid-Western Educational Research Association, Columbus, OH, Oct. 15-18.

MERTLER C A, 2009. Teachers' assessment knowledge and their perceptions of the impact of classroom assessment professional development [J]. Improving schools, 12(2): 101-113.

MERTLER C A, CAMPBELL C S, 2004. Assessing those who assess: development of an instrument to measure teachers' assessment literacy[C]. Paper presented at the Annual Meeting of the Mid-Western Educational Research Association, Columbus, OH, Oct. 13-16.

MERTLER C A, CAMPBELL C S, 2005. Measuring teachers' knowledge &. application of classroom assessment concepts: development of the "Assessment Literacy Inventory"[C]. Paper presented at the Annual Meeting of the American Educational Research Association, Montreal, Quebec, Canada, Apr. 11-15.

MILLER M D, LINN R L, GRONLUND N E, 2009. Educational testing and assessment: context, issues, and trends[M]//Linn R L. Measurement and assessment in teaching. New Delhi: Pearson Education: 1-25.

MORRISON J A, LEDERMAN N G, 2003. Science teachers' diagnosis and understanding of students' preconceptions [J]. Science education, 87(6): 849-867.

MUÑOZ A P, PALACIO M, ESCOBAR L, 2012. Teachers' beliefs about assessment in an EFL context in Colombia[J]. Profile: issues in teachers' professional development, 14(1): 143-158.

NEESOM A, 2000. Report on teachers' perceptions of formative assessment[R]. London: QCA.

NITKO A J, BROOKHART S M, 2007. Education assessment of students (5th ed.)[M]. Upper Saddle River: Prentice Hall.

O'LOUGHLIN K, 2006. Learning about second language assessment: insights from a postgraduate student on-line subject[J]. University of Sydney papers in TESOL, 1: 71-85.

O'SULLIVAN R G, JOHNSON R L, 1993. Using performance assessments to measure teachers' competence in classroom assessment[C]. Paper presented at the Annual Meeting of the American Educational Research Association, Atlanta, GA, Apr. 12-14.

O'LOUGHLIN K, 2013. Developing the assessment literacy of university proficiency test users[J]. Language testing, 30(3): 363-380.

PAJARES M F, 1992. Teachers' beliefs and educational research: cleaning up a messy construct[J]. Review of educational research, 62(3): 307-332.

PASTORE S, ANDRADE H L, 2019. Teacher assessment literacy: a three-dimensional model[J]. Teaching and teacher education, 84: 128-138.

PAVLENKO A, 2007. Emotions and multilingualism [M]. Cambridge: Cambridge University Press.

PILL J, HARDING L, 2013. Defining the language assessment literacy gap: evidence from a parliamentary inquiry[J]. Language testing, 30(3): 381-402.

PLAKE B S, IMPARA J C, FAGER J J, 1993. Assessment competencies of teachers: a national survey[J]. Educational measurement: issues and practice, 12(4): 10-12.

POEHNER M E, 2008. Dynamic assessment: a Vygotskian approach to understanding and promoting L2 development (Vol. 9)[M]. New York: Springer.

POPHAM W J, 2004. Curriculum, instruction, and assessment: amiable allies or phony friends? [J] Teachers college record, 106(3): 417-428.

POPHAM W J, 2008. Transformative assessment[M]. Alexandria, VA: ASCD.

POPHAM W J, 2009. Assessment literacy for teachers: faddish or fundamental? [J]. Theory into practice, 48(1): 4-11.

POPHAM W J, 2011a. Assessment literacy overlooked: a teacher educator's confession[J]. The teacher educator, 46(4): 265-273.

POPHAM W J, 2011b. Transformative assessment in action—an inside look at the applying process[M]. Alexandria, VA: ASCD.

POPHAM W J, 2018. Assessment literacy for educators in a hurry [M]. Alexandria, VA: ASCD.

QUILTER S M, 1998. In-service teachers' assessment literacy and attitudes toward assessment [D]. University of South Carolina, Columbia.

QUILTER S M, CHESTER C, 1998. In-service teachers' perceptions of educational assessment[C]. Paper presented at the Annual Meeting of the Mid-Western Educational Research Association, Chicago, IL, Oct. 14-17.

QUILTER S M, GALLINI J K, 2000. Teachers' assessment literacy and attitudes[J]. The teacher educator, 36(2): 115-131.

REA-DICKINS P, 2008. Classroom-based language assessment[M]// Shohamy E, Hornberger N. Encyclopedia of language and education (Vol. 7). New York: Springer: 257-272.

REMESAL A, 2007. Educational reform and primary and secondary teachers' conceptions of assessment: the Spanish instance, building upon Black and Wiliam[J]. The curriculum journal, 18(1): 27-38.

REMESAL A, 2011. Primary and secondary teachers' conceptions of assessment: a qualitative study[J]. Teaching and teacher education, 27 (2): 472-482.

REYNOLDS-KEEFER L, 2010. Rubric-referenced assessment in teacher preparation: an opportunity to learn by using [J]. Practical assessment, research, and evaluation, 15: Article 8.

ROHL M, 1999. Profiling ESL children: how teachers interpret and use national and state assessment frameworks[J]. Queensland journal of educational research, 15(1): 113-122.

SADLER D R, 1998. Formative assessment: revisiting the territory [J]. Assessment in education: principles, policy & practice, 5(1): 77-84.

SATO M, WEI R C, DARLING-HAMMOND L, 2008. Improving teachers' assessment practices through professional development: the case of National Board Certification[J]. American educational research journal, 45(3): 669-700.

SCARINO A, 2013. Language assessment literacy as self-awareness: understanding the role of interpretation in assessment and in teacher learning[J]. Language testing, 30(3): 309-327.

SCARINO A, 2014. Learning as reciprocal, interpretive meaning-making: a view from collaborative research into the professional learning of teachers of languages[J]. The modern language journal, 98(1): 386-401.

SCHAFER W D, LISSITZ R W, 1987. Measurement training for school personnel recommendations and reality [J]. Journal of teacher education, 38(3): 57-63.

SCHUMANN J H, 1997. The neurobiology of affect in language: a supplement to language learning[M]. Malden, MA: Blackwell.

SERPIL Ö Z, ATAY D, 2017. Turkish EFL instructors' in-class language assessment literacy: perceptions and practices[J]. ELT research journal, 6(1): 25-44.

SHEPARD L A, 2006. Classroom assessment[M]//Brennan R L. Educational measurement (4th ed.). Westport: Praeger: 623-646.

SHEPARD L A, HAMMERNESS K, DARLING-HAMMON L, et al. 2005. Assessment [M]//Darling-Hammond L, Bransford J. Preparing teachers for a changing world: what teachers should learn and be able to do. San Francisco, CA: Jossey-Bass: 201-231.

SHOHAMY E, 1998. Critical language testing and beyond [J]. Studies in educational evaluation, 24(4): 331-345.

SHOHAMY E, 2001. Democratic assessment as an alternative[J].

Language testing, 18(4): 373-391.

SHOHAMY E, INBAR-LOURIE O, POEHNER M, 2008. Investigating assessment perceptions and practices in the advanced foreign language classroom [R]. University Park, PA: Center for Advanced Language Proficiency Education and Research, Report No. 1108.

SIEGEL M A, WISSEHR C, 2011. Preparing for the plunge: pre-service teachers' assessment literacy [J]. Journal of science teacher education, 22(4): 371-391.

SKEHAN P, 1998. A cognitive approach to language learning[M]. Oxford: Oxford University Press.

SMITH K, 2011. Professional development of teachers—a prerequisite for AfL to be successfully implemented in the classroom[J]. Studies in educational evaluation, 37(1): 55-61.

STABLER-HAVENER M L, 2018. Defining, conceptualizing, problematizing, and assessing language teacher assessment literacy[J]. Studies in applied linguistics and TESOL, 18(1): 1-22.

STERN H H, 1983. Fundamental concepts of language teaching[M]. Oxford: Oxford University Press.

STIGGINS R J, 1991. Assessment literacy[J]. Phi delta kappan, 72 (7): 534-539.

STIGGINS R J, 1995. Assessment literacy for the 21st century[J]. Phi delta kappan, 77(3): 238-254.

STIGGINS R J, 1999. Are you assessment literate? [J]. High school magazine, 6(5): 20-23.

STIGGINS R J, 2004. New assessment beliefs for a new school mission[J]. Phi delta kappan, 86(1): 22-27.

STIGGINS R J, 2008. Assessment manifesto: a call for the development of balanced assessment systems [R]. Portland, OR: ETS Assessment Training Institute.

STIGGINS R J, 2009. Assessment for learning in upper elementary grades[J]. Phi delta kappan, 90(6): 419-421.

STIGGINS R J, 2010. Essential formative assessment competencies for teachers and school leaders [M]//Andrade H, Cizek G. Handbook of formative assessment. New York: Routledge: 233-250.

STIGGINS R J, CHAPPUIS J, 2005. Using student-involved classroom assessment to close achievement gaps[J]. Theory into practice, 44(1): 11-18.

STIGGINS R J, ARTER J A, CHAPPUIS J, et al. 2004. Classroom assessment for student learning: doing it right, using it well (2nd ed.) [M]. Portland: Assessment Training Institute, Inc.

STIGGINS R J, DUFOUR R, 2009. Maximizing the power of formative assessments[J]. Phi delta kappan, 90(9): 640-644.

TAYLOR L, 1997. Developing learning in professional education: partnerships for practice[M]. New York: McGraw-Hill Education.

TAYLOR L, 2009. Developing assessment literacy[J]. Annual review of applied linguistics, 29: 21-36.

TAYLOR L, 2013. Communicating the theory, practice and principles of language testing to test stakeholders: some reflections[J]. Language testing, 30(3): 403-412.

TIERNEY R D, 2006. Global/Cultural teachers creating possibilities: reading worlds, reading selves, and learning to teach[J]. Pedagogies, 1 (1): 77-87.

TSAGARI D, VOGT K, 2017. Assessment literacy of foreign language teachers around Europe: research, challenges and future prospects [J]. Papers in language testing and assessment, 6(1): 41-63.

VANDEYAR S, KILLEN R, 2007. Educators' conceptions and practice of classroom assessments in post-apartheid South Africa[J]. South African journal of education, 27(1): 101-115.

VOGT K, TSAGARI D, 2014. Assessment literacy of foreign language teachers: findings of a European study[J]. Language assessment quarterly, 11(4): 374-402.

VOLANTE L, FAZIO X, 2007. Exploring teacher candidates' assessment literacy: implications for teacher education reform and professional development[J]. Canadian journal of education, 30(3): 749-770.

WALTERS F S, 2010. Cultivating assessment literacy: standards evaluation through language-test specification reverse engineering [J]. Language assessment quarterly, 7(4): 317-342.

WANG T H, WANG K H, HUANG S C, 2008. Designing a web-based assessment environment for improving pre-service teacher assessment literacy[J]. Computers & education, 51(1): 448-462.

WEIR C, KHALIFA H, 2008. A cognitive processing approach towards defining reading comprehension[J]. Cambridge ESOL: research notes, 31: 2-10.

WILIAM D, 2010. The role of formative assessment in effective learning environments [M]//Dumont H, Istance D, Benavides F. The nature of learning: using research to inspire practice. Paris: OECD: 135-155.

WILLIS J, ADIE L, KLENOWSKI V, 2013. Conceptualising teachers' assessment literacies in an era of curriculum and assessment reform[J]. The Australian educational researcher, 40(2): 241-256.

WININGER S R, NORMAN A D, 2005. Teacher candidates' exposure to formative assessment in educational psychology textbooks: a content analysis[J]. Educational assessment, 10(1): 19-37.

WINKE P, GOERTLER S, 2008. Did we forget someone? Students' computer access and literacy for CALL[J]. CALICO journal, 25(3): 482-509.

WYATT-SMITH C, GUNN S, 2009. Towards theorising assessment as critical inquiry [M]//Wyatt-Smith C, Cumming J J. Educational assessment in the 21st century. Dordrecht: Springer: 83-102.

WYATT-SMITH C, KLENOWSKI V, GUNN S, 2010. The centrality of teachers' judgement practice in assessment: a study of standards in moderation[J]. Assessment in education: principles, policy & practice, 17(1): 59-75.

XU Y T, BROWN G T L, 2016. Teacher assessment literacy in practice: a reconceptualization[J]. Teaching and teacher education, 58: 149-162.

XU Y T, BROWN G T L, 2017. University English teacher assessment literacy: a survey-test report from China[J]. Papers in language testing and assessment, 6(1): 133-158.

XU Y T, HE L Y, 2019. How pre-service teachers' conceptions of assessment change over practicum: implications for teacher assessment literacy[J/OL]. Frontiers in education, 4: 145[2021-12-1]. https://doi.org/10.3389/feduc.2019.00145.

XU Y T, LIU Y C, 2009. Teacher assessment knowledge and practice: a narrative inquiry of a Chinese college EFL teacher's experience [J]. TESOL quarterly, 43(3): 492-513.

YAN X, ZHANG C, FAN J S, 2018. "Assessment knowledge is important, but...": how contextual and experiential factors mediate assessment practice and training needs of language teachers[J]. System, 74: 158-168.

YONG A G, PEARCE S, 2013. A beginner's guide to factor analysis: focusing on exploratory factor analysis [J]. Tutorials in quantitative methods for psychology, 9(2): 79-94.

ZHANG Z C, BURRY-STOCK J A, 1997. Assessment practices inventory: a multivariate analysis of teachers' perceived assessment competency[C]. Paper presented at the Annual Meeting of the National Council on Measurement in Education, Chicago, IL, March 25-27.

ZHANG Z C, BURRY-STOCK J A, 2003. Classroom assessment practices and teachers' self-perceived assessment skills [J]. Applied measurement in education，16（4）：323-342.

ZIMINA E V，2018. Teacher involvement in the Russian national exam in foreign languages：experience and perspectives［M/OL］//Xerri D，Briffa P V. Teacher involvement in high-stakes language testing. Cham：Springer：245-261［2021-2-21］. https：//doi. org/10. 1007/978-3-319-77177-9_14

蔡金亭，2019. 外语学习中的母语迁移［N/OL］. 中国社会科学报：12-31［2021-11-2］. http：//www. cssn. cn/zx/ bwyc/201912/t20191231_5068030. shtml.

戴水姣，史小平，2015. 高校"国培计划"课程设置的思考——以小学英语教师培训课程为例［J］. 大学教育科学（06）：68-73.

傅春晖，2010. 外语课堂评价理论与实践［M］. 湘潭：湘潭大学出版社：102.

金艳，2018. 外语教师评价素养发展：理论框架和路径探索［J］. 外语教育研究前沿，1（02）：65-72＋93.

李细妹，2020. 评估儿童语言学习者［D］. 广州：广东外语外贸大学.

李筱菊，1997. 语言测试的科学与艺术［M］. 长沙：湖南教育出版社.

李亮，王蔷，2020. 外语教师课堂评价素养：概念构成、观测体系及实践启示［J］. 外语测试与教学（02）：20-27.

林敦来，2016. 中国中小学英语教师评价素养研究［M］. 北京：人民大学出版社.

林敦来，2019. 中小学英语教师语言评价素养参考框架［M］. 北京：外语教学与研究出版社.

林敦来，高淼，2011. 教师评估素养：理论与实践［J］. 外语教学理论与实践（04）：29-37.

刘建达，2018. 中国英语能力等级量表与英语测评［J］. 中国考试（11）：1-6.

刘建达，贺满足，2020. 语言测试效度理论的新发展［J］. 现代外语，43（04）：565-575.

南纪稳，2016. 教师评价素养的现状、问题与提升策略［J］. 教师教育论坛，29(06)：21-24＋32.

潘鸣威，2020. 外语教师语言测评素养再探——基于对语言测试专家的访谈[J]. 中国考试(07)：34-41.

彭小虎，王国峰，朱丹，2014. 儿童发展与教育心理学[M]. 上海：华东师范大学出版社.

乔晨丽，2017. 城镇高中英语教师评价素养研究[D]. 西安：西安外国语大学.

秦晓晴，2009. 外语教学问卷调查[M]. 北京：外语教学与研究出版社.

邵雯，2015. 职前与在职中学英语教师语言评价素养培训需求调查研究[D]. 广州：广东外语外贸大学.

舒涵影，2018. 国内大学英语教师语言测评素养调查研究[D]. 广州：广东外语外贸大学.

王初明，1991. 外语学习中的认知和情感需要[J]. 外语界(04)：7-11.

王媛媛，2018. 基于结构方程模型的重庆市中学英语教师语言评价素养研究[D]. 重庆：西南大学.

王怡楠，2019. 初中英语教师课堂评价素养研究[D]. 昆明：云南师范大学.

吴明隆，2010. 问卷统计分析实务——SPSS操作与应用[M]. 重庆：重庆大学出版社：221-235.

杨帆，吴莎，2018. 测评、教学与学习的衔接——第三届语言测试与评价国际研讨会暨第五届英语语言测评新方向研讨会述评[J]. 中国考试(02)：71-77.

张淼，2020. 初中英语教师评价素养研究[D]. 重庆：重庆三峡学院.

赵雪晶，2014. 我国中学教师教学评价素养研究[D]. 上海：华东师范大学.

郑东辉，2009. 教师评价素养发展研究[D]. 上海：华东师范大学.

郑东辉，叶盛楠，2012. 中小学教师课堂评价知识及其来源的研究——基于浙江省的样本调查[J]. 教育发展研究，32(20)：68-78.

郑瑶，2020. 学科核心素养背景下的初中英语教师评价素养研究[D]. 厦门：集美大学.

Appendix Ⅰ   Expert Judgement of the LAL Measuring Instrument for Primary and Middle School EFL Teachers

Distinguished experts,

This questionnaire aims to gather your opinions about a measuring tool targeting primary and middle school (including junior and senior) EFL teachers' language assessment literacy(LAL). You are sincerely invited to rate the extent to which the items are aligned with the LAL definition and theoretical model. Your suggestions of revision are warmly welcome. All your responses will be anonymous. Thanks very much for your participation.

Directions: In this questionnaire, a five-point Likert rating scale is used to indicate the extent to which you agree with each question. Please highlight the rating that best represents your opinions.

1. Definition of LAL

LAL for Chinese EFL teachers is defined as "a set of knowledge, skills, and principles that they need in order to assess effectively students' language learning in relation to the learning objectives, language use abilities, and capacity for language learning, and to provide immediate, appropriate, and useful feedback to them". Specifically, an assessment literate Chinese EFL teacher:

(1) is familiar with language learning objectives against which to assess students;

（2）is familiar with the various components of language knowledge and ability and understands how these components are developed；

（3）is aware of students' cognitive and affective characteristics in language teaching and assessment；

（4）understands student' language learning processes and their capacity for language learning；

（5）is familiar with assessment processes and different assessment methods；

（6）is aware of the principles and ethic considerations that guide language assessments；

（7）is skilled in choosing, designing, and scoring classroom language assessments and communicating assessment results appropriately to pupils and their parents；

（8）gets students to involve in assessments；

（9）assesses effectively students' language learning outcomes and gives them a sense of progression；

（10）provides timely and useful feedback to students；and

（11）makes evidence-informed adjustments in instruction and facilitates students' learning.

2. LAL model

LAL is conceptualized as a dynamic construct which involves the knowledge, skills, and principles components.

Knowledge：
- knowledge of assessment in language pedagogy
- knowledge of linguistics and applied linguistics
- awareness of students'cognitive and affective characteristics（in language teaching and assessment)

Skills：
- technical skills in assessment

Principles：

　　• assessment principles & ethic considerations

3. LAL survey instrument

　　Directions: There are a total of 41 items in the LAL instrument targeting primary and middle school EFL teachers' expertise in each LAL component. These items overlap to some extent and are put under the dimension they are most relevant to.

　　Dimension 1: assessment in language pedagogy
　　(1) how to use assessments to evaluate progress in language learning
　　(2) how to use assessments to evaluate achievement in language learning
　　(3) how to use assessments to diagnose learners' strengths and weaknesses
　　(4) how to use assessments to motivate students to learn
　　(5) how to involve students in assessment
　　(6) how to use classroom assessment to maintain pupils' interest in language learning
　　(7) how to provide useful feedback to pupils after assessment
　　(8) how assessments influence teaching and learning in the classroom
　　(9) how to prepare students for assessment
　　(10) how to make use of assessment evidence to adjust language teaching
　　(11) how to make use of assessment evidence to help students set learning goals
　　(12) how to make use of assessment evidence to push students forward toward their learning goals

　　3-1) To what extent do you agree with the items under this dimension of **assessment in language pedagogy**?

Strongly disagree	Disagree	Undecided	Agree	Strongly agree
1	2	3	4	5

3-2) Can you suggest some changes to these items and explain your reasons for proposing them?

Dimension 2: technical skills in assessment

(13) selecting appropriate items or tasks for a particular assessment purpose

(14) developing good quality language assessment items/tasks

(15) explaining assessment tasks to students

(16) developing portfolio-based assessments

(17) making decisions about what aspects of language to assess

(18) evaluating the quality of language tests

(19) communicating assessment results to students or parents

(20) interpreting what a particular score says about an individual's language ability

(21) developing marking schemes for productive language assessments

(22) communicating assessment decisions to students or parents

3-3) To what extent do you agree with the items under this dimension of **technical skills in assessment**?

Strongly disagree	Disagree	Undecided	Agree	Strongly agree
1	2	3	4	5

3-4) Can you suggest some changes to these items and explain your reasons for proposing them?

Dimension 3: knowledge of linguistics and applied linguistics

(23) the various components of language ability

(24) how language knowledge develops

(25) how language skills develop

(26) how students learn a foreign language

(27)students' capacity for learning the foreign language

(28)overall language learning objectives in *National English Curriculum Standards*

(29)overall language learning objectives in the teaching syllabus

(30)the CSE (China's Standards of English Language Ability) descriptors of language proficiency at different grade levels

3-5) To what extent do you agree with the items under this dimension of knowledge of **linguistics and applied linguistics**?

Strongly disagree	Disagree	Undecided	Agree	Strongly agree
1	2	3	4	5

3-6) Can you suggest some changes to these items and explain your reasons for proposing them?

Dimension 4: assessment principles & ethic considerations

(31)test reliability

(32)test validity

(33)different purposes of language tests (e. g. achievement, diagnosis)

(34)fair treatment of every student in assessment

(35)how to identify bias in language assessments

3-7) To what extent do you agree with the items under this dimension of **assessment principles & ethic considerations**?

Strongly disagree	Disagree	Undecided	Agree	Strongly agree
1	2	3	4	5

3-8) Can you suggest some changes to these items and explain your reasons for proposing them?

Dimension 5: knowledge of students' cognitive and affective characteristics

(36) children's growth in cognitive, social, emotional, and physical aspects

(37) children's development of literacy in their first language

(38) children's literacy in the foreign language

(39) children's vulnerability to criticism and failure

(40) how to align language assessment tasks with the curriculum and syllabuses

(41) how to align language assessment tasks with the CSE (China's Standards of English Language Ability)

3-9) To what extent do you agree with the items under the dimension of **knowledge of students' cognitive and affective characteristics**?

Strongly disagree	Disagree	Undecided	Agree	Strongly agree
1	2	3	4	5

3-10) Can you suggest some changes to these items and explain your reasons for proposing them?

_____

3-11) To what extent do you agree with the entire questionnaire?

Strongly disagree	Disagree	Undecided	Agree	Strongly agree
1	2	3	4	5

3-12) Can you suggest some changes to the questionnaire and explain your reasons for proposing them?

_____

Thanks again for your participation.

Appendix Ⅱ   Questionnaire on Primary and Middle School EFL Teachers' Assessment Knowledge, Skills, and Practices

Dear teachers,

Thank you very much for your participation. This survey focuses on your assessment-related knowledge and skills and on how you conduct assessment practices in classroom. It takes about 15 minutes to complete, and there are no right or wrong answers. Your responses are restricted for research purposes and will be kept confidential. Please be honest with your answers.

Directions: In this survey, assessments are not confined to tests, but include the various instructional and assessment activities that classroom teachers use to measure students' learning, such as questioning, classroom observations, seatwork, role plays, discussions, after-class assignments, portfolios, self-assessment, and peer-assessment.

Ⅰ. Assessment-related Knowledge

Directions: Questions 1-19 focus on your assessment-related knowledge. To what extent are you knowledgeable of the answer to each question? Please select from 1-5 the option that best corresponds to you.

1: unknowledgeable   2: slightly knowledgeable

3: moderately knowledgeable   4: very knowledgeable

5: extremely knowledgeable

1. How to use assessments to diagnose students' learning difficulties?

◯1   ◯2   ◯3   ◯4   ◯5

2. What teaching methods are effective for English instruction?

◯1   ◯2   ◯3   ◯4   ◯5

3. How to use varied assessment methods (e. g. portfolios, self-assessment, and peer-assessment)?

◯1   ◯2   ◯3   ◯4   ◯5

4. How does your school assess students' English learning, both formatively and summatively?

◯1   ◯2   ◯3   ◯4   ◯5

5. What skills are included under the umbrella term language skills?

◯1   ◯2   ◯3   ◯4   ◯5

6. How to choose/design appropriate instructional activities to help students learn language points?

◯1   ◯2   ◯3   ◯4   ◯5

7. How to assess students' learning via routine instructional activities?

◯1   ◯2   ◯3   ◯4   ◯5

8. How to use assessments to record students' progress?

◯1   ◯2   ◯3   ◯4   ◯5

9. In addition to knowledge of phonetics, grammar, and vocabulary, what else is included under the umbrella term language knowledge?

◯1   ◯2   ◯3   ◯4   ◯5

10. How to use assessments to measure students' mastery of the teaching content?

◯1   ◯2   ◯3   ◯4   ◯5

11. How to use assessments to motivate students to learn English?

◯1   ◯2   ◯3   ◯4   ◯5

12. How to design instructional activities to enhance students' language skills?

◯1   ◯2   ◯3   ◯4   ◯5

13. How to get students to involve in peer-assessment or self-assessment? (For instance, what other materials do teachers need to prepare for

students to assess peers or themselves, in addition to the task itself?)

○1   ○2   ○3   ○4   ○5

14. <u>For primary and junior middle school English teachers:</u> What are the overall goals of the English curriculum as stipulated in the *English Curriculum Standards for Compulsory Education*?

<u>For senior middle school English teachers:</u> What are the overall goals of the English curriculum as stipulated in the *English Curriculum Standards for General High School*?

○1   ○2   ○3   ○4   ○5

15. What is the structure of language? (i. e. the hierarchical order of language, e. g. phoneme, word, …)

○1   ○2   ○3   ○4   ○5

16. What are the local education authority's requirements or regulations with regards to the testing of students' English learning? (e. g. What is emphasized in the test, language knowledge or language skills? What language skills need to be covered in the test?)

○1   ○2   ○3   ○4   ○5

17. <u>For primary and junior middle school English teachers:</u> What are the overall requirements of assessment specified in the *English Curriculum Standards for Compulsory Education*? (e. g. Who is the agent of assessment? How to assess student learning? What should be the focus in assessment, language knowledge or language abilities?)

<u>For senior middle school English teachers:</u> What are the overall requirements of assessment specified in the *English Curriculum Standards for General High School*? (e. g. Who is the agent of assessment? How to assess student learning? What should be the focus in assessment, language knowledge or language abilities?)

○1   ○2   ○3   ○4   ○5

18. According to *China's Standards of English Language Ability* (issued in 2018), what general language abilities do your students need to possess when they graduate?

○1   ○2   ○3   ○4   ○5

19. In addition to its influence on English pronunciation, how does our native language (Chinese) influence our English learning?

○1   ○2   ○3   ○4   ○5

Ⅱ. Assessment-related Skills

Directions: Questions 20 ~ 30 focus on your assessment-related skills. Please select from 1~5 the option that best corresponds to you.

1: very untrue of me   2: essentially untrue of me
3: undecided   4: essentially true of me
5: very true of me

20. I am able to be consistent in marking/grading. (i. e. I will give approximate scores to similar responses.)

○1   ○2   ○3   ○4   ○5

21. I am able to describe language test results(e. g. computing the average score, the high and low, and the number of students in a particular range).

○1   ○2   ○3   ○4   ○5

20. I am able to make inferences about how effective students are in their language learning based on their assessment results.

○1   ○2   ○3   ○4   ○5

21. I am able to communicate test results to students and their parents in an appropriate way.

○1   ○2   ○3   ○4   ○5

22. I can make performance standards appropriate to students' language proficiency. (For instance, students of different grades vary in their language abilities. I can make appropriate standards to assess their listening and speaking skills.)

○1   ○2   ○3   ○4   ○5

23. I am able to communicate assessment purposes and procedures to

students clearly.

○1   ○2   ○3   ○4   ○5

24. I can make general inferences about students' language use abilities according to their assessment results. (For instance, what kind of materials can they comprehend? What language functions can they perform with English?)

○1   ○2   ○3   ○4   ○5

25. I can help students to make adjustments in their learning strategies based on their assessment results.

○1   ○2   ○3   ○4   ○5

28. I can provide timely and appropriate feedback to students according to assessment results (e. g. what are their strengths and weaknesses? How to improve their weak areas?).

○1   ○2   ○3   ○4   ○5

29. I can make adjustments in instruction based on assessment results (e. g. adjusting teaching pace, teaching methods, and instructional activities).

○1   ○2   ○3   ○4   ○5

30. I can make inferences about students' capacity for English learning based on their assessment results.

○1   ○2   ○3   ○4   ○5

III. Assessment-related Practices

Directions: Questions 31~62 focus on your assessment-related practices. Please select from 1~5 the option that best corresponds to you.

1: very untrue of me   2: essentially untrue of me

3: sometimes untrue and sometimes true of me

4: essentially true of me   5: very true of me

31. I design a variety of assessment activities so that students can demonstrate their language knowledge and skills to a fuller extent.

○1   ○2   ○3   ○4   ○5

32. I take into account students' daily performance when marking. (For instance, I will be more lenient with weak students so as not to demotivate them, and I will be more harsh with top students so that they will not take excessive pride in themselves.)

  ○1   ○2   ○3   ○4   ○5

33. When designing assessment activities, I only choose those materials that are relevant to students' life.

  ○1   ○2   ○3   ○4   ○5

34. I make reflections on my teaching processes based on assessment results.

  ○1   ○2   ○3   ○4   ○5

35. When designing assessments, I will choose assessment tasks of which the difficulty is a little bit above students' language abilities.

  ○1   ○2   ○3   ○4   ○5

36. More often than not, I encourage students when I provide feedback to them about their performance on assessment tasks.

  ○1   ○2   ○3   ○4   ○5

37. I am not concerned about the deviation of students' scores when I describe language test results.

  ○1   ○2   ○3   ○4   ○5

38. I motivate students to learn in my classroom.

  ○1   ○2   ○3   ○4   ○5

39. I use specific and vivid teaching aids to assist my English teaching.

  ○1   ○2   ○3   ○4   ○5

40. In my classroom, students are allowed to use Chinese if they can not complete the assessment task with English.

  ○1   ○2   ○3   ○4   ○5

41. When designing teaching activities, I think about how to make students have a sense of progression in English learning.

  ○1   ○2   ○3   ○4   ○5

42. When designing tests, I would write a few test items beyond the scope

of the curriculum/syllabus to meet the needs of some top students.

○1   ○2   ○3   ○4   ○5

43. I spend much time in classroom to strengthen students' mastery of English knowledge and skills.

○1   ○2   ○3   ○4   ○5

44. I give mild criticism to those students who do not perform well on assessments.

○1   ○2   ○3   ○4   ○5

45. I protect students' privacy to test scores and rankings.

○1   ○2   ○3   ○4   ○5

46. For primary English teachers: I prepare students to take end-of-term examinations.

For middle school English teachers: I prepare students to take Zhongkao/Gaokao.

○1   ○2   ○3   ○4   ○5

47. I award low scores as a punishment to those students who hold a negative attitude towards English learning.

○1   ○2   ○3   ○4   ○5

48. In classroom, I design instructional activities to check students' learning.

○1   ○2   ○3   ○4   ○5

49. I avoid culturally inappropriate content in my assessments.

○1   ○2   ○3   ○4   ○5

50. I mainly use tests to gather information about students' learning.

○1   ○2   ○3   ○4   ○5

51. I make adjustments in assessment tasks according to students' learning status, e. g. raising or lowering the difficulty of assessment tasks.

○1   ○2   ○3   ○4   ○5

52. I use tasks approximate in form to instructional activities to assess students.

○1   ○2   ○3   ○4   ○5

53. I give fair treatment to every student in assessment.

    ○1   ○2   ○3   ○4   ○5

54. I evaluate students' learning after a unit of instruction.

    ○1   ○2   ○3   ○4   ○5

55. When designing assessment tasks, I will think about the alignment between assessment content and the teaching objectives.

    ○1   ○2   ○3   ○4   ○5

56. I develop assessment methods appropriate for instructional decisions.

    (**Example for primary English teachers**: When checking whether pupils know the pronunciation of a specific letter or letter combination, teachers can ask pupils to select from the glossary those words which contain the target letter/letter combination that is pronounced as specified, rather than ask pupils to write such words.

    Example for middle school English teachers: When checking whether students master the use of a specific tense (e. g. the past tense) in a quick fashion, teachers can develop MC items or fill-in items to achieve this purpose, rather than ask them to write a short passage using the target tense.

    ○1   ○2   ○3   ○4   ○5

57. I place more weightings on tasks that measure students' general language use abilities when designing tests.

    ○1   ○2   ○3   ○4   ○5

58. When designing assessment activities, I will think about the extent to which the assessments can measure students' mastery of the teaching content.

    ○1   ○2   ○3   ○4   ○5

59. I will make adjustments in assessment tasks for those students with disabilities or other learning impairments.

    ○1   ○2   ○3   ○4   ○5

60. I will help students to set up learning goals based on their assessment results.

○1　　　　○2　　　　○3　　　　○4　　　　○5

61. I can articulate the specific learning objectives of the unit I am teaching.

○1　　　　○2　　　　○3　　　　○4　　　　○5

62. I use assessments to make comparisons between students.

○1　　　　○2　　　　○3　　　　○4　　　　○5

IV. Background Information

63. Your geographic area: City _____ , Province _____

64. Gender: ○ male　○ female

65. Years of teaching:

　○ Less than 5 years

　○ 5～10 years

　○ 11～15 years

　○ 16～20 years

　○ More than 20 years

66. Have you ever received any education or training in educational assessment (including language assessment)?

　○ Yes　　　　　　　○ No

67. Highest academic degree

　○ Associate degree

　○ Bachelor

　○ Master

　○ Others

68. Your grade level of teaching:

　○ Primary school

　○ Junior middle school

　○ Senior middle school

69. Geographic area of the school you work at:

　○ Rural area

　○ County town

　○ Urban area

70. Factors that affect your assessment practices:

○ Work load (weekly teaching hours)

○ Class size

○ Assessment knowledge and skills

○ Assessment requirements imposed by the school

○ Availability of technical support

○ Students' willingness to cooperate

○ Other factors, please specify _____.

Thanks again for four support and cooperation. Wish you stay healthy and enjoy a happy life.

Appendix Ⅲ　Final Rotated Pattern Matrix
（Formal Survey）

Item	Factor				
	1	2	3	4	5
Item 38	. 654				
Item 39	. 651				
Item 36	. 470				
Item 8		−. 636			
Item 7		−. 621			
Item 2		−. 619			
Item 1		−. 597			
Item 11		−. 589			
Item 10		−. 573			
Item 6		−. 557			
Item 13		−. 540			
Item 3		−. 508			
Item 12		−. 493			
Item 4		−. 479			
Item 22			−. 741		
Item 26			−. 682		
Item 30			−. 646		
Item 20			−. 625		
Item 27			−. 622		

（Continued）

Item	Factor				
	1	2	3	4	5
Item 29			−.605		
Item 23			−.603		
Item 21			−.595		
Item 24			−.593		
Item 25			−.572		
Item 28			−.535		
Item 58				.638	
Item 59				.624	
Item 62				.529	
Item 55				.510	
Item 57				.481	
Item 61				.463	
Item 60				.447	
Item 53				.422	
Item 14					−.690
Item 15					−.688
Item 17					−.586
Item 9					−.571
Item 19					−.568
Item 5					−.406
Item 18					−.404